Collective Bargaining and the Academic Librarian

by

JOHN W. WEATHERFORD

The Scarecrow Press, Inc.

Metuchen, N.J.   1976

ISBN 0-8108-0983-4

Library of Congress Catalog Card No. 76-45424

CONTENTS

48374

PREFACE

This study has several origins. One lies in my contact with faculty collective bargaining. That contact began in
1971 when I was one of six negotiators chosen to bargain on
behalf of Central Michigan University its second agreement
with the NEA-affiliated Faculty Association. When this agreement expired three years later, I was again summoned to the
bargaining table; and when economic issues were re-opened
in the following year I was to my surprise asked once again
to serve. This year I chair the team. I have never sought but
never regretted this role. It has consumed some fifteen months
of the past six years, but the experience has been educational
and expanding. I felt that I was learning things of interest to
many but known to few, and wished to share them.

As a Council on Library Resources Fellow in 1973, I
was able to visit a score of four-year institutions or systems
to observe the impact of actual bargaining on academic librarians. I am indebted to CLR for its provision of travel
expenses for this purpose. I am indebted to Central Michigan
University for having granted the necessary leave to pursue
the CLR project, but this gratitude extends also to particular
members of its administration. The unreserved support of
Dr. Charles Ping, then provost of Central and now president
of Ohio University, was essential and gratifying. So too was
the assistance of Dr. William Boyd, then president of Central
and now president of the University of Oregon; of Dr. Neil

Bucklew, then vice-provost and chief negotiator, and now provost of Ohio University; and of J. David Kerr, university legal counsel for Central. Each has contributed to the literature in this fresh field of faculty bargaining, and association with them has been stimulating.

My visits, subsequent communication with other practitioners in many states, and various experiences as a library director, suggested that many librarians and classroom faculty members were unfamiliar with important aspects of faculty bargaining. Little wonder, for as recently as 1970 only two of the four-year institutions had concluded faculty union agreements.

Thus this is a primer of collective bargaining for the faculty in general, with special emphasis on academic librarians. It is not meant to sway anybody for or against any union, or for or against collective bargaining. I have tried to present both sides, but not at the cost of suppressing my own viewpoint. Between adversaries there is always some hope of conciliation, and indeed bargaining is founded on this hope. The two sides will not achieve sound conciliation by pretending that they do not have differences.

John W. Weatherford

GUIDE TO ACRONYMS

AAUP	American Association of University Professors
ACBIS	Academic Collective Bargaining Information Service
ACRL	Association of College and Research Libraries
AFT	American Federation of Teachers
AGB	Association of Governing Boards
ALA	American Library Association
APSCUF	Associated Pennsylvania State College and University Faculties
CAUT	Canadian Association of University Teachers
CPI	Consumers' Price Index
CUNY	City University of New York
CUPA	College and University Personnel Association
ICLE	Institute for Continuing Legal Education
LACUNY	Library Association of the City University of New York
LAUC	Library Association of the University of California
LRRM	Labor Relations Reference Manual
MEA	Michigan Education Association
MERC	Michigan Employment Relations Commission
NCSCBHE	National Center for the Study of Collective Bargaining in Higher Education
NEA	National Education Association
NJEA	New Jersey Education Association

NJFT	New Jersey Federation of Teachers
NLRB	National Labor Relations Board
NYU	New York University
OPEIU	Office and Professional Employees' International Union
PERC	Public Employment Relations Commission
PNLA	Pacific Northwest Library Association
SPA	Senate Professional Association
SUNY	State University of New York
SUNYLA	State University of New York Library Association
UFCT	United Federation of College Teachers

Chapter 1

INTRODUCTION

Librarians bargain collectively through many agents and under many conditions throughout the United States, and with ever greater variety throughout the world. Nevertheless, this study of mature bargaining relationships involving librarians in four-year colleges and universities of the United States is not as narrow as the description might suggest. There are, after all, over 60,000 such faculty members and related bargaining unit members, including (at a very rough guess) 2,000 professional librarians.[1] The boundaries just described may be explained as follows.

"Mature bargaining relationships" is my not-too-arbitrary description of the stage of relationship in which formal collective bargaining has produced a written agreement between the parties. It was important to limit the study in this manner because there seemed no other way of wading through the fluid speculations surrounding unionization. The proof is in the pudding alone.

"Librarians" generally means professional librarians, though here and there individual staff members for historical reasons are so listed without meeting the usual requirements.

"Four-year colleges and universities" distinguishes these librarians from those experiencing different conditions and bargaining situations in industrial, government, school, and public libraries. These, as we shall see, have little in common with academic librarians respecting collective bargaining. Even two-year colleges prove on examination to have more in common with the schools. Some, far from being distinguished from K-12 systems, are part of K-14 systems.

"United States" is a limitation somewhat regretfully imposed. Canadian academic librarians have traveled a path apart from the Americans. Their experience gives us refreshing perspectives through contrast, just as ours should give them. British and more exotic examples are even more difficult to incorporate.

Development of Faculty Bargaining

Because nearly all of the academic librarians involved are part of a bargaining unit comprising mostly classroom faculty, faculty bargaining and working conditions perforce concern much of this study. This faculty association need not be the only one available to academic librarians, and in fact it may be unavailable to them some day when they would prefer it; yet so far the bargaining histories of the two groups have been inextricably commingled.

The first formal collective bargaining involving college faculty occurred in the two-year colleges in 1965, spreading to include 56 of them by 1970. Although the four-year institutions soon followed, the progress of bargaining was much slower. By 1970, only two of these had actually bargained agreements: CUNY (unionized in 1968) and Central Michigan University (unionized in 1969). By the following year, however, the number had reached seventeen and many more were by then in process. This growth followed legislation in such labor states as New York, Michigan, Pennsylvania, Rhode Island, and New Jersey permitting public employees to engage

in collective bargaining. Supplementing these developments
in public institutions, the National Labor Relations Board in
1970 assumed jurisdiction over private colleges or universities having annual budgets of over $1,000,000, and thus
permitted their faculties to bargain also. By 1974, about
half of the four-year institutions with faculty agreements were
private, though the greater number of persons were in the
public institutions. By June 1975, faculty on 157 four-year
campuses had adopted bargaining agents, and 37 had rejected
them.[2] Such figures are useful only to convey a general im-
pression, as they are necessarily in constant flux. They
show a continuing if irregular growth of collective bargaining
among four-year faculties. On each such campus it has
variously affected the character of the institution and the
lives of faculty and administrators.

System and Campus

The geographical scope of bargaining profoundly affects
the nature of the relationship between institution and union,
and the sensitivity of the process to local feelings. A majority of American faculty members in bargaining units belong to state systems. Their bargaining agent represents the
whole system, and their employer for bargaining purposes is
either a state system headquarters or the governor. Thus
the State University of New York, comprising twenty four-
year and six two-year colleges, bargains with the United University Professionals (NEA-AFT), and the agreement binds
every campus. In the New Jersey system of eight colleges,
the New Jersey Board of Higher Education and the governor's
labor relations representative bargain with the American Federation of Teachers. Again, the central agreement binds all
campuses. The Pennsylvania State College system comprises

fourteen colleges, and the state department of education bargains a single agreement with an NEA affiliate, the Association of Pennsylvania State College and University Faculties.
Smaller state college systems in Vermont and Nebraska follow similar patterns. Of all these state systems, only SUNY
is comprehensive, covering a wide range of institutions. The
rest are partial systems made up of institutions of similar
mission and background--largely teachers' colleges, or former teachers' colleges recently expanded.

The City University of New York is a comprehensive
system with a wide variety among its twelve four-year and
eight two-year colleges. CUNY bargains with the Professional Staff Congress, a single agent representing the faculty and
related employees (now affiliated with AFT).

Massachusetts, too, has a state college system, but
here each college is treated separately. Some have AFT,
some NEA, and some do not engage in collective bargaining.
Nevertheless, each agent bargains with administrative teams
selected by the system, and the resulting agreement, though
peculiar to each campus, to a large extent represents the
stance of the system headquarters. For this reason, the
agreements, though not uniform, bear certain marked similarities. Even the bargaining units are not all the same,
and Lowell State excluded librarians from the faculty unit.

The two four-year public campuses of Rhode Island
bear a similar relation to the state. The faculty of the University of Rhode Island have an AAUP agent, and those of
Rhode Island College an AFT agent, and each has its own
agreement. The bargaining, however, is conducted at the
state level with the deputy commissioner of education.

Beyond the systems lie a number of public four-year
institutions that bargain locally and produce agreements of

great variety.

Legislation

The geography of faculty bargaining can be drastically altered from 1976 on by various legislative developments. At present, all but the smallest private institutions can bargain under the aegis of the National Labor Relations Board, but bargaining in public institutions is largely dependent on the existence of state legislation. Occasionally employer and agent agree to bargain voluntarily in states without bargaining legislation for public employees, as in Montana, Kansas, Maryland, and Ohio. More often, bargaining relationships in the public sector mature only in the presence of state regulation. Thus at this time a considerable pressure appears to be dammed up in the public colleges and universities of states that have no such legislation. Over twenty states without such legislation are considering bills. They differ in important matters such as the bargainability of certain issues. [3]

Approximately half of the states at this writing had laws explicitly or implicitly covering collective bargaining in public higher education. In seven states, some bargaining is occurring without legislative provision, most notably in Ohio. In about fifteen states that have legislation, faculties of public four-year colleges or universities have either bargained agreements or have at least been formed into bargaining units. In all but the deep South, those states that in 1974 did not have legislation permitting public employee bargaining had bills pending to do so. Since then, some have succeeded and some have failed: yet another figure in constant flux.

Superimposed on this complex prospect of numerous

and varying state laws is the possibility of federal legislation which would not only permit bargaining in states that do not have legislation, but would regulate public employee bargaining in the states that do. In the latter case, such legislation could be favorable in one state and unfavorable in another to existing union interests. At this writing it is too early to speculate on proposed federal legislation.

The Unions

Faculty collective bargaining in the United States is dominated by three great national affiliations: the American Association of University Professors, the American Federation of Teachers, and the National Education Association. As of mid-1975, their respective successes numbered as follows:

Union	Four-year institutions			Four-year campuses
	All	Public	Private	
AAUP	29	12	17	34
AFT	17	9	8	26
NEA	24	16	8	46
AAUP/AFT merger	1	1	0	1
AAUP/NEA merger	1	1	0	2
AFT/NEA merger	7	3	4	39
Independent	9	3	6	9
TOTAL	88	45	43	157

At that time, only ten of these institutions were "research universities" (using AAUP's long-established classification), and for these the only bargaining agent was AAUP (except for University of Hawaii faculty, who are represented by AAUP/NEA).

During the same time, the faculties of 37 four-year institutions formally voted to reject collective bargaining. Of these, ten are "research universities."[4]

All three of the national organizations have long histories, the AAUP dating from 1915, AFT from 1916, and NEA from 1857. Only of the AFT can it be said that "From the beginning it stressed the adversary relationship between teachers and administrators," and only AFT began with the intention of bargaining collectively.[5] When in the 1960s higher education faculty entered bargaining, the AFT was first in recruiting them. It was, in fact, in response to AFT competition that the NEA entered bargaining. The NEA and AFT have a particular interest in the teachers' colleges. From these colleges come the new school teachers who may themselves be voting in certification elections in the elementary and secondary schools. Thus NEA-AFT competition in higher education has been an extension of K-12 competition. For both, the overwhelming bulk of dues and members comes from the public schools.

The national AAUP responded reluctantly to collective bargaining, adopting it only in 1972 as a "major additional means" of achieving existing AAUP goals.[6] Nevertheless, by 1975 AAUP had been elected the bargaining agent in 29 four-year institutions, compared to 24 for NEA, 17 for AFT, 9 coalitions, and 9 independent unions.

Nationally these organizations show philosophical differences. The AAUP, for example, declares support for the traditional powers of the senate; AFT and NEA have no national policy statements regarding traditional governance.[7] Their views on tenure differ. All oppose quotas. AAUP prefers applying strict standards for awarding tenure, and maintains its long-standing distinction between the untenured and tenured conditions. NEA, on the other hand, regards tenure as a right of anyone achieving certain minimum qualifications, and favors a short probation period. AFT does not appear to have enunciated a national policy regarding tenure.

The three national organizations used widely different expressions in describing their attitudes towards the strike as a weapon in bargaining. AFT candidly supports strikes, though as a last resort. NEA originally opposed but in 1968 withdrew its formal stand in the face of their use by its own local unions. AAUP sounds extremely reluctant to strike, on a cursory reading of its policy, which limits this sanction to "extraordinary situations which so flagrantly violate academic freedom or the principles of academic government, or which are so resistant to rational methods of discussion, persuasion, and conciliation, that faculty members may feel impelled to express their condemnation by withholding their services," and to cases in which they believe that the administration "is inflexibly bent on a course which undermines an essential element of the educational process."[8] Another equally fair reading of this policy, however, can justify strikes if the other side seems unreasonable--and of course the other side usually does. This broad latitude is reflected in actual experience; of the four major faculty strikes, one (New Jersey state colleges) has been by AFT and three by AAUP: St. John's, Rider, and Oakland.

Actual agreements show little if any uniformity or pattern imposed by these national or state union offices. NEA in 1970 produced a model contract for colleges, drawing on its experience in elementary and secondary schools, but the model seems to have had little effect anywhere in higher education.[9] Local conditions rather than national policies govern both union demands and the final agreement. Furthermore, the faculty may choose an agent for reasons other than its proclaimed philosophy. Thus a group sympathetic with AAUP might support AFT on a theory that AFT would wield greater power and still, under their own tutelage, pursue AAUP goals.

If we do not forget the primacy of local concerns, we can indulge in a few generalities about the three national union affiliations. For AFT especially, bargaining is bargaining in any employment situation including higher education, and the faculty should concentrate on successful traditional bargaining to achieve their ends. AFT is sometimes regarded as more "militant," perhaps only because of its long-standing and frank insistence on the adversary employer-employee relationship. AFT is part of AFL-CIO and has its roots in the labor movement. The roots of NEA lie in secondary and elementary education. In higher education, its major appeal as a bargaining agent has been to the faculties of teachers' colleges. AAUP differs from AFT and NEA in having never represented any group except college and university professors. Its appeal to the research universities so far is unmistakably stronger than that of the rival unions. In bargaining, AAUP local chapters/unions sometimes show a keener sense of traditional faculty power, whether to preserve it or to expand it.

Causes of Faculty Bargaining

It is speculative to suggest the causes for college and university professors suddenly turning to collective bargaining fifty years after the birth of the youngest of these three organizations. Job security looms large as a probable motive.

In 1971, Gus Tyler could write, "For the untenured, the union is an instrument to negotiate job security in whatever form."[10] Several others have identified the same motive. By 1973, however, job security had become a disturbing issue for the tenured as well as the untenured, as they discerned what Garbarino has called "the ominous trends in the supply and demand for potential faculty" and the "end of affluence."[11] Undoubtedly they also discerned all too easily the reversal of an earlier tendency of faculty salaries to outrun prices.

Even before these general economic difficulties, other influences were playing more subtly on faculties. The growth of program budgeting introduced the notion of an accountability which applied to the academic world criteria which were notoriously non-academic and threatening to faculty predominance in choosing goals and means in education and research. Pressure came not only from bureaucrats, donors, and legislators (liberal and conservative), but, in their own terms, from another quarter: students. Some states, in the same context, centralized and bureaucratized their colleges and universities, reflecting a faith in the efficacy and economy of the large scale. Their purpose was greater uniformity; the effect was to threaten the power, autonomy and individuality of the professoriate who had, not by chance, chosen this highly individualistic calling.[12] Here then is a development remarkably similar to that observed by Guyton in his study of some public librarians' attitudes towards collective bargaining.[13] The imposition of alien standards produced alienation.

Insecurity of employment, of status, and of independence are surely plausible enough reasons for faculties to seek relief through novel means such as collective bargaining.

When a vote favors its adoption by a hair's breadth, who knows how influential any one consideration may be? Local experiences are critical. The vote at Temple has been attributed at least in part to the radicalization of non-tenured faculty by the climax of the Vietnam episode during the Nixon administration.[14] It has been said, too, that in one former teachers' college those who embraced it first were the older education faculty, defending their status from the newly-imported young faculty in social and exact sciences; but in another college the reverse was the case.[15] Several AAUP reports of the grosser violations of academic freedom or of due process prove to have occurred at institutions that soon after adopted collective bargaining. Where traditional processes appear inadequate to preserve basic faculty roles and rights, the burden of proof may shift in faculty minds, so that for them it behooves tradition and not the union to prove its superiority. Nor can sheer indignation be ignored. Though in the whole of academe censurable actions may be rare, they offend the community of scholars; and particularly on the campus where the offense has occurred, it is not surprising if the faculty seek successive means of redress until they find one that works. One means often available in the sixties was to get a better job elsewhere, but now declining mobility places greater pressure on other means.

Faculty desires for security, money, individuality, and fair process may thus ignite collective bargaining, but it is not the faculty alone who fuel its progress. Struggles between employer and bargaining agent are not the only stresses increased or relaxed by bargaining. It fortifies the convictions of any management that sees virtue in centralization. The belief of unions, that in union there is strength, cannot be all that alien to a state agency that sees

individual colleges and universities each making separate
settlements. To the vexed question of how much autonomy
a public college or university should exercise, the local
president and local faculty may offer the same answer in
favor of autonomy; but where systems exist, central bargaining transfers further management powers to headquarters. Central collective bargaining is a way for a central
management to assert or increase its power over individual
state institutions. Thus we come full circle, to find that
the bureaucratization that helped cause faculty unionism
seems to be thriving on the resultant bargaining relationship.

The Process

Faculty members can bargain collectively for their
immediate working conditions, such as compensation, job
security, promotion, or grievance procedures. They may
also have societal interests and concerns which are such
vivid features of their intellectual environment that they regard them as working conditions. Orthodox bargaining distinguishes between familiar working conditions and these
other features. Thence arise frustrations and conflict.
Some concerns are not mandatory subjects of bargaining,
such as the selection of management personnel, tuition
rates, the budget, or the manner in which an agreement is
ratified. Some concerns are illegal to bargain, such as a
demand to contravene affirmative action or equal employment
opportunity requirements. There is, too, a great grey area
in which the obligation to bargain is uncertain. [16]

These questions of bargainability are important, but
what is more basic to a general understanding of the process
is to realize that neither side necessarily gets what it bargains for. This is a good time to outline the usual steps

of the process:

1) A group of employees petitions to hold an election on whether to have a bargaining agent, and on what the agent is to be.

2) A bargaining unit is established either by agreement with the employer or by a labor board, describing the exact group of employees to vote in the election and to be represented by a successful agent.

3) If the petition includes a certain requisite number of the potential bargaining unit members, the election or elections are held.

4) The agent and the employer notify each other of the areas in which they propose to bargain.

5) Negotiators representing each side must meet at reasonable times to receive demands and bargain. The two sides have to bargain in good faith on all mandatory subjects contained in their demands and offers. They do not have to reach agreement.

6) If they do not reach agreement, they are then at an impasse. Depending on the jurisdiction, parties at impasse may have their differences evaluated by a neutral mediator or fact-finder, or resolved by an arbitrator. Normally the arbitrator's task in this circumstance is to choose one or the other of the parties' last offers. Sometimes impasse results in a strike. Generally strikes are legal in private institutions and illegal in public ones, though in some states it is difficult to enforce a prohibition against an illegal strike.

7) If, on the other hand, the negotiators reach agreement, they are to reduce it to writing. The union ratifies the agreement according to its own by-laws, which may require approval by the whole bargaining unit, or only

by dues-paying members, or even by smaller groups such as the union executive board. After union ratification, management ratifies. If ratification fails on either side, bargaining is normally resumed. [17]

The bargaining process as just described is an adversary system. It depends on each side negotiating for the interests of its own constituency. It differs from war, minimally in that it operates within rules enforced by superior and external power, and hopefully in that it is moderated by the knowledge of both sides that their relationship must continue to be constructive down the years despite the stresses of negotiation. An adversary relation need not be hostile, though in truth it often is so. What is called union-management cooperation is really a channeling of the adversary process, through lessened hostility and heightened trust, towards some mutually desirable end. In public higher education, for instance, there is a theoretical opportunity for the adversaries to cooperate in lobbying for greater fiscal support. This study concentrates on the adversary relation, divorced from its hostilities, because it seems convenient to show the frame of bargaining, and let readers plaster it with their own emotions and involvements. In any case, a study of hostilities would require a different set of knowledge, methods, and perceptions. Bargaining is an irrational process insofar as it resolves disputes by reference to power of some kind (e.g., legal and fiscal penalties, lockouts, strikes, picketing, recruitment of public opinion, or the threat of a sullen faculty). In fairness to bargaining, it should be said that the disputes themselves are not as antiseptic as they may seem. For example, the reasonable proposition that faculty participation is essential to the welfare of students may be a facade for plainer

motives based on anger because president X is a pompous
autocrat, or business manager Y runs the university, or
union leader Z is a megalomaniac.

Academic Librarians

No standard treatment characterizes the librarians of
academe, either in absolute terms or in relation to classroom faculty. In any aspect of working conditions, the
faculty are a more homogeneous population than are the
academic librarians, a fact only confirmed by the efforts of
ACRL to establish standards. [18]

There has been no comprehensive study of the working conditions of the academic librarian, but examining collective bargaining makes us consider them more critically
than has been done. Irrational though bargaining may be at
its extremes, it does impose a more austere discipline of
thought and a firmer command of facts, particularly as the
other side may perceive them. Now for librarians collective
bargaining is a cold light raking their aspirations and assumptions. In this light "faculty status" ceases to be a neat
entity and disintegrates into components that must be exam-
ined severally. The truth of a colleague relationship between
librarians and classroom teachers is not to be judged by
membership in the faculty club. Even the conjunction of librarians and professors in the common bond of grievance
procedure or of a strike is somehow less demonstrative of
"faculty status" when the same bond also embraces laboratory technicians and graduate assistants.

Or again: How are librarians to attain professional
advancement? Should they even seek advancement through
achievement instead of the step system and the common
rule? How would librarians play a game in which the

strategic choices were to join a unit of library employees, or of faculty members, or of librarians only, or of non-classroom professionals? How many hours a week does a professional employee work? Should librarians fight, join, or ignore such traditional faculty power nodes as the academic senate?

The chapters which follow are devoted primarily to the situations in which academic librarians may find themselves in the presence of collective bargaining. To many it will seem strange to hear these situations described now in faculty terms and now in labor terms, but where librarians and faculty are joined in bargaining, faculty and labor terms are the new composite language by which their condition is to be described.

Notes

1. The National Center for the Study of Collective Bargaining in Higher Education produces a quarterly report of current developments: "Higher Education Institutions with Collective Bargaining Agents." ACBIS produces similar reports; the latest at this writing was Edward P. Kelley, Jr., ACBIS Special Report no. 12 (Update) (July 1975) 18 pp. The Chronicle of Higher Education also keeps its readers current regularly throughout the year on the institutions and agents that have engaged in collective bargaining. See also Bill Aussieker and Joseph W. Garbarino, "Measuring Faculty Unionism: Quantity and Quality," Industrial Relations, 12 (May 1973) 117-124. Obviously such figures are updated constantly by all means available, so that sources on the topic are soon superseded. For the rough estimate of librarians involved, compare institutions in this situation with U.S.O.E. Library Statistics, 1972-1973.

2. The historical developments are traced briefly in Daniel R. Coleman, "The Evolution of Collective Bargaining As It Relates to Higher Education in America," CUPA Journal, 23 (March 1972) 40-60; and in

"Academic Collective Bargaining: History and
Present Status," Item 1 of ACBIS Orientation
Packet (February 1975) 2 pp.

3. Thomas Emmet and Doris Ross, "1975 Legislative
    Activity: Progress Report on Postsecondary Col-
    lective Negotiation Bills," ACBIS Special Report
    no. 21 (April 1975) 8 pp. Also: J. David Kerr,
    "Pending Federal Legislation Providing State Public
    Employee Collective Bargaining," paper presented
    at the National Association of College and Univer-
    sity Administrators, 1975. Processed, 16 pp. Al-
    so, National Education Association, Government Re-
    lations, Legislative Analysis. "Collective Bargain-
    ing for Public Employees ... H. R. 77 (March 25,
    1975)." Processed, 3 pp.

4. Aussieker and Garbarino, loc. cit. Also, "Collective
    Bargaining on Campuses," Chronicle of Higher Edu-
    cation (June 9, 1975) 5.

5. "Faculty Professional Associations," Item 5 of ACBIS
    Orientation Packet (December 1973) 7 pp. Also
    Daniel R. Coleman, "The Evolution of Collective
    Bargaining As It Relates to Higher Education in
    America," CUPA Journal, 23 (May 1972), 4-5.

6. Ibid.

7. Ibid.

8. Ibid.

9. Ralph S. Chesebrough and Philip A. Encinio, "Sample
    Contract...." National Society of Professors,
    1970. n. p.

10. Gus Tyler, "The Faculty Join the Proletariat," Change,
    3 (Winter, 1971-72) 44.

11. Joseph W. Garbarino, "Precarious Professors: New
    Patterns of Representation," Industrial Relations,
    10 (February 1971), 1-20. Also, Coleman, op.
    cit. , (March 1972), 4-2.

12. Joseph Garbarino and Bill Aussieker, "Faculty Union-
    ism: From Theory to Practice," Industrial

Relations, 11 (February 1972) 1-21. Also Garbarino, (February 1971), and Coleman loc. cit.

13. Theodore Lewis Guyton, Unionization: The Viewpoint of Librarians. A. L. A., 1975. 204 pp.

14. Ellis Katz, "Faculty Stakes in Collective Bargaining: Expectations and Realities," in Jack H. Schuster, ed., Encountering the Unionized University. Issue 5 of New Directions for Higher Education (Spring, 1974) 30.

15. Garbarino, (February 1972), 3.

16. J. David Kerr and Kenneth Smyth, "Bargaining Issues," in Terrence N. Tice, ed., Faculty Power: Collective Bargaining on Campus Institute of Continuing Legal Education, Ann Arbor, 1972. 368 pp. 315-317.

17. Neil S. Bucklew, "Unionized Students on Campus," Educational Record, 54 (Fall, 1973) 300, gives a useful summary of the process that differs in detail from this. For faculty strikes, see C. Gregory Lozier, "Changing Attitudes Towards the Use of Strikes in Higher Education," CUPA Journal, 25 (April 1974) 41-48. Also, James P. Begin, Theodore Settle, and Paula Alexander, Academics on Strike. Institute of Management and Labor Relations (Rutgers), and ACBIS, 1975. 135 pp.; and H. L. Nixon, "Faculty Support of Traditional Labor Tactics on Campus," Sociology of Education, 48 (Summer, 1975) 276-286.

18. John Weatherford, "Librarians in Faculty Unions," Library Journal, 99 (October 1, 1974) 2443-2446.

Chapter 2

COMPENSATION

Economic issues dominate collective bargaining in general, and it is rare for them to be excluded entirely, as they were for a time among the Massachusetts state colleges. One writer has suggested a reciprocal relation between economic and non-economic goals in faculty bargaining. If inflation is severe enough, unions forego the faculty-power target for the money target; and if college and university administrators can spare the price, they offer money in preference to new extensions of faculty power.[1] The same Massachusetts colleges that did not bargain money bargained instead what is probably the most complete revision to date of traditional governance. Our times, however, have been characterized by both inflation and a scarcity of money. The resulting penury of both sides protracts and embitters negotiations which at best show more equality than fraternity.

Comparison

It is natural to seek comparisons of the compensation of faculty who have collective bargaining and those who do not, and of faculty and librarians. Unfortunately not much light has been shed on these questions. One study shows that the choice of a particular national affiliation (AAUP,

AFT, NEA) has had no effect on salary increases. [2] Birnbaum estimates that from 1968-69 to 1972-73, faculty members under collective bargaining had achieved $740 more in
individual annual compensation than those not under it. [3]
Much has happened since 1972-73 to make further investigation desirable.

It is not easy to make such comparisons, curious as
we may be about them. Comparisons may always be clouded
by the question of whether the level of non-union compensation is raised by union successes ("spillover" in the jargon).
Moreover, the formal compensation of an employee comprises, beyond salary, ingredients with monetary values
contingent on certain events, such as illness, accident,
pregnancy, death, or even too-long life. These are fringe
benefits, though popular usage extends the term to joys that
are not all bargainable, such as climate, culture, housing,
and civic order. Salaries are often less than 80% of one's
compensation, the exact proportion varying from system to
system and even from person to person within a system.
The mean proportion of salary to compensation for all faculty
in the United States declined from 94% in 1965-66 to 84%
in 1974-75. [4] Some compensation items are funded by salary
deductions at one place and by institutional contributions at
another. Some are taxable one way and not the other.
Fringes become more important as one ascends the economic
scale. Beginners need cash, but those in higher tax brackets prefer to be rewarded in ways that do not require a
heavy tribute to Caesar. Librarians and teachers may tell
each other at conventions that they have "full health coverage" and be communicating less than they suppose. One
health insurance plan may cover some continued disability,
some kinds of psychiatric care, and alcoholism. Another

may not cover these troubles; may have a ceiling so low
that protection ends just when it is needed most; may en-
tangle its transactions in red tape; and may be unpopular
among physicians, unfamiliar outside of one state, and rid-
dled with exceptions that surface only at billing time. There
are other possible differences, but the two may still be
called "full health coverage." Similarly, retirement, disability, and life insurance plans are not readily comparable.

Living in an expensive or inexpensive community also
affects our comparisons of income. The AAUP salary sur-
veys attempt to meet this need, though their regions ("New
England," "Middle Atlantic," and so forth) are too large and
heterogeneous. [5] Much of salary bargaining is colored by the
"cost of living" index. This usually refers to figures published by the Bureau of Labor Statistics, giving the price of
a certain constant market basket of goods and services. [6]
The contents of this ideal market basket were selected originally in 1957 and revised in 1967-68. The basket contains
about 400 items that urban wage-earners and clerical workers
might normally be expected to buy. The price of this basket
has come to be called the "cost of living." The index looms
large in negotiations with employees of all sorts. It is not
necessarily an accurate measure of the needs of a faculty.
The basket holds no educational costs, for example, and the
index therefore fails to reflect one onerous burden on some
faculty families. On the other hand, a majority of faculty
members enjoy incomes higher than that of the family that
buys the B. L. S. basket. What faculty members do with the
extra income is not just to buy more of the same basket,
but to save, or spend in areas not represented by the index.
It is perhaps melodramatic to refer to all of these other
areas as a "cost of living."

Inflation is not a monopoly of the faculty. Custodians, clerks, and others, often in bargaining units of their own, suffer inflation as well. Beyond them, the university or college must cope with inflation as the cost of books, electricity, microscopes, and scores of other essentials rise. [7]

Among four-year institutions, the C. P. I. has been used only by Regis College as an agreed factor in actually determining salary increases. Central Michigan, in a former agreement, provided that salaries could be bargained anew at the request of either side if the C. P. I. strayed more than 15% above or below its level at the time the agreement was signed. [8] Despite the rarity of cost-of-living clauses, the index has contributed richly to the rhetoric of bargaining, and sometimes to the philosophy of income distribution.

Distribution

When collective bargaining arrives on campus, it finds an existing salary structure which may or may not be systematic, and superimposes increases on the structure, modifying rather than replacing it.

Union demands reflect internal political pressures, and these sometimes seek to reduce the difference between the highest and the lowest salaries in the bargaining unit. One way to move towards this end is to express all salary increases as an equal amount of dollars for each member of the unit. Although the difference in dollars between highest and lowest remains exactly the same, the impact on the employees is greater at the lower end of the scale. At $10,000 a year, a $600 raise is 6%; at $30,000, only 2%, and in any case the $600 probably means more subjectively to the former case. Salary increases may also be expressed

as graduated increments of dollars, such as $600 for those
making less than $12,000 a year; $500 for those making
$12,000 to $14,999; and so on, truly compressing the
range. A less predictable variant in academe gives graduated increases according to rank. A graduated scale of
percentage increases can be made to compress the range;
for example, 6.5% for the lowest bracket, 6% for the next
lowest, and so on. Another element that tends to compress
the range by lifting the lower-paid at the expense of the
higher is the establishment of minima for each rank. The
impact of the floor system depends of course on the level of
the minima. On the other hand, a salary increase that is
expressed as a uniform percentage stretches out the range.
On $10,000, 6% is a $600 raise; on $30,000, 6% is an
$1,800 raise. Proponents of compressed pay scales would
argue that this example gives $1,200 to somebody who needs
it least, by taking it from somebody who needs it most.

Salaries may also be shown in tables establishing the
salary uniformly paid to employees according to rank and
number of years in that rank. This is the step system.
At its most rigid it sets maximum as well as minimum
salaries, and does not permit adjustments to compete in the
market place for particular skills or knowledge. Not infrequently the difference between one academic rank and the
next higher is the same in dollars as the difference between
the first year in rank and the fourth or fifth, so that the
reward for meeting promotion criteria is equal to the reward for having started three or four years earlier and not
meeting them.

Salaries can be further modified in individual cases
by "merit pay" and "inequity adjustments." We are such
slaves of our own jargon that we have come to treat these

as competing concepts, as if equity were the opposite of
merit.

Academic promotions represent a merit system of
long standing, where they have not been vitiated by the in-
jection of seniority as a major criterion. Otherwise, merit
systems have tended to allocate a sum (say 1% of the compensation of the whole bargaining unit) for distribution at
discretion according to meritorious performance. This discretion may be exercised by deans, colleagues, or a union-
administration committee. Merit pay is more often given as
a bonus than as a continuing addition to base pay. Merit
rewards have not been common in faculty bargaining, but
they exist at SUNY and Wayne, and formerly existed at Central Michigan. At least the AFT and NEA unions are hostile
to merit systems. [9]

"Inequity adjustments" have become popular with the
growth of affirmative action for the fair treatment of women
and minorities. Collective bargaining has made useful
progress in pursuing fairness, usually by allocating a sum
to a joint committee which is charged to study and seek out
local inequities, and to remedy them as far as the money
permits. Not every method, unfortunately, identifies un-
fairness. For example, one factor in calculating "inequity"
is sometimes the number of years that a person has spent
in an academic rank. It is therefore possible for one person
to be rewarded under the familiar promotion system for
meeting those criteria which colleagues and institution had
identified as desirable, and for another person to be rewarded under the new inequity adjustment for not having met
them, if his or her failure has extended over a long enough
span of years. Theoretically at least, the booby prize can
exceed first prize. As this particular kind of inequity

adjustment, if persevered in, flattens and equalizes the reward system, it is probably more accurate to call them inequality adjustments. It is not certain that their benefit to
genuine inequity cases, the women and minorities whom they
were meant to help, outweighs the bounty that they bestow
upon white males of modest attainment.

Salary increases need not rest on a single factor
and, in fact, combinations are not unusual. An agreement
may set a percentage increase, add a fixed dollar amount
to that, and then undergird both with a minimum salary for
each academic rank. Here are some examples of typical
salary bargains:

1. Step system (e. g. , Pennsylvania state colleges, CUNY, and Southeast Massachusetts).

2. Equal dollar distribution (e. g. , Ferris).

3. Uniform percentage distribution (e. g. , New
   Jersey state colleges, SUNY, and Rutgers).

4. Mixed dollar and percentage distribution (e. g. ,
   Central Michigan, Ferris, and Temple).

5. Floors other than step system (e. g. , Central
   Michigan, Ferris, and Temple).

6. Merit (e. g. , Temple, SUNY, and Wayne).

7. Inequity (e. g. , SUNY, Central Michigan,
   Temple, and Wayne).

The agreements show a few salary manipulations that
are unusual but of general interest. Central Michigan has
an achievement award system that funds individual faculty
projects, which differs from merit pay in that the emphasis
is on the merit of the project rather than the record of the
applicant. Oakland included among its salary variables a
multiplier ("department-school factor") meant presumably

to reflect the market. The following are a few examples: art is given a factor of 1.018; mathematics, 1.095; English, 1.022. Economics and management are the highest, at 1.170, and librarians are the lowest, at 1.010. The Temple agreement responds to the market problem by permitting the University to match a rival offer if it desires.

It has been convenient to speak of salary changes as increases. It is of course quite possible to bargain salary decreases. The mechanics would be the same as those discussed.

Librarians

Librarians have been beneficiaries of faculty collective bargaining through a process that has been described as follows: "What had been a series of relatively separate occupational labor markets is being merged into one larger academic professional market.... The paradox of faculty unionism to date is that the greatest gains have accrued to the teaching faculty on the margin of the core faculty ... and to non-faculty professionals."[10]

Salary comparisons are vexed by the ambivalence of the profession in evaluating and equating nine-month, ten-month, and eleven-month work years. We all know that $14,000 for a nine-month year is better than $14,000 for an eleven-month year, but we do not agree on how much better it is. To some, the nine-month year is a way of life that they would not sell for a two-ninths increase in compensation, and their view is fortified by the workings of the income tax. Others would prefer to be able to convert the short year to the long year at will, and collect their two-ninths.

Librarians on year-round contract are unequally treated by any distribution that does not prorate their increases, as at Ferris, where the nine-month faculty and eleven-month librarians each received the same total increase ($700 in 1973-74 and $840 in 1974-75).

Differences in the fringe benefits of librarians and faculty have virtually disappeared under faculty bargaining. Some pay systems, still, are better for librarians, as librarians with faculty rank tend to cluster in the ranks of instructor and assistant professor, and in any case are typically paid less than the classroom faculty.[11] Thus a salary system that compresses the whole range improves the position of librarians in faculty units. If librarians tend to stay in rank, they have little reason to look to promotion as a way to improve their lot, though to be sure they have an interest in establishing criteria that open their way to promotion. A system (e.g., steps) that rewards employees for the number of years they have spent in one rank places a greater proportion of salary increases in the hands of librarians.

So does the setting of minimum salaries for each rank. To illustrate, let us see what Central Michigan's 1972-73 salary floors would have done for the salaries of the non-supervisory librarians of similar institutions reported by Cameron and Heim for the same year.[12] These Central Michigan floors for ten-month faculty, including librarians, were:

Professor	$15,900
Associate	12,700
Assistant	10,800
Instructor	8,800

Let us suppose that Cameron and Heim's non-supervisory

librarians were all instructors, and had year-round contracts, which by Central Michigan policy would be convert-
ible to 11/9 of $8,800, or $10,756. Let us also suppose
that the mean salary of each reported level was midway in
the bracket (i. e. , the mean of the $6,000-$6,999 bracket
was $6,500, etc.). The following table shows the propor-
tion of librarians in the lower salary brackets of the Cameron and Heim survey, and the increases that they would
have experienced had these floors been established at all of
their "similar" institutions:

Salary bracket	6000-6999	7000-7999	8000-8999	9000-9999
Librarians in bracket	3%	10%	19%	18%
Central Mich. 11-month floor	10,756	10,756	10,756	10,756
Increase to reach floor	65%	43%	27%	13%

Of course regional and other differences prevent any such
extremities as these from materializing, though if some of
Cameron and Heim's librarians were assistant professors
(and of course some were) the increases would be even
greater. The purpose of the illustration is merely to show
the mechanical effect of salary floors on librarians in faculty bargaining units. In actual situations, floors have had
substantial impact on librarians' salaries, and for a very
few librarians they have increased salaries by 30% to 40%.

Some librarians complain, after having risen with a
floor, that they are still on the floor after it has risen.
That is how this system works. The economic exhilarant
may thus be a spiritual depressant, depending on whether we

compare where we are with where we were, or with where others are. An increase in floors is sometimes greater and never less than other increases in its effect on the individual, for if other increases do not bring the salary to the minimum, the minimum prevails.

Our only experience so far has been of librarians in faculty bargaining units. [13] Members of a single bargaining unit need not be treated equally in the settlement. At Wayne the classroom faculty are paid according to academic rank, and other unit members according to job classification, the librarians' salaries running close to those of the counseling service. Librarians are paid under different schedules from the faculty in the Southeastern Massachusetts agreement and in the New Jersey state tables.

Nevertheless, the more common pattern in bargained agreements has been to apply the same salary changes to librarians as to classroom faculty. As noted earlier, these changes are usually superimposed on an existing system, in which librarians are paid less than classroom teachers. Certain changes modify the system in favor of librarians. Librarians have received little direct attention in salary bargaining. It is perhaps as well for them, for their greatest gains have come incidentally from systems designed for the whole faculty. How academic librarians would fare alone or in league with non-teaching professionals we do not yet know. The patterns that we have observed demonstrate the paramount importance to librarians of the composition of the bargaining unit.

Notes

1. Robert Birnbaum, "Unionization and Faculty Compensation," Educational Record, 55 (Winter, 1974) 29-33.

2. Virginia Lee Lussier, "National Faculty Associations in Collective Bargaining: A Comparative Discussion," ACBIS Special Report No. 8 (n. d.) 21 pp. 6-7.

3. Birnbaum, loc. cit. See also his "The Effects of Collective Bargaining on Faculty Compensation in Higher Education," in National Center for the Study of Collective Bargaining in Higher Education. Second Annual Conference (April, 1974) 83-96. Recent studies of schoolteachers' compensation have produced some controversy over whether unionization has improved compensation or has had no effect on it. See: G. Alan Balfour, "More Evidence That Unions Do Not Achieve Higher Salaries for Teachers," Journal of Collective Negotiations in the Public Sector, 3 (1974) No. 4, pp. 289-304; Gary A. Moore, ". . . Comment," JCNPS, 4 (1975) No. 3, pp. 253-256; and Thomas A. Brown, "Have Collective Negotiations Increased Teachers' Salaries?" JCNPS, 4 (1975) No. 1, pp. 53-66.

4. "Two Steps Backward. Report on the Economic Status of the Profession, 1974-75," AAUP Bulletin, 61 (Aug. , 1975) 119-199. p 127.

5. Ibid. Information also printed and graphed in Chronicle of Higher Education (June 9, 1975) 8-10.

6. U. S. Bureau of Labor Statistics. CPI Detailed Report for July 1975. Consumer Price Index, U. S. and City Averages. Sept. 1975. See also Richard Bronstein, "Cost of Living and Salary Administration," Personnel, 52 (March-April, 1975) 11-18, for more detail on how to interpret C. P. I.

7. William G. Bowen, "The Effects of Inflation/Recession on Higher Education," Educational Record, 56 (Summer, 1975) 149-155.

8. Thomas Mannix, "Prospective Issues at the Bargaining Table," ACBIS Special Report No. 19 (March, 1975) 6 pp. For a recent overview, see Audrey Freedman, "Cost-of-Living Clauses in Collective Bargaining," Michigan Business Review, 27 (Jan. , 1975) 6-11.

9. Everett C. Ladd, Jr. and Seymour M. Lipset, "Unionizing the Professoriate," Change, 5 (Summer, 1973) 42.

10. Joseph W. Garbarino, "Faculty Unionism: From Theory to Practice," Industrial Relations, 11 (Feb., 1972) 15.

11. Donald F. Cameron and Peggy Heim, Librarians in Higher Education. Their Compensation Structure for the Academic Year 1972-73. Council on Library Resources, 1974. 24 pp. For an earlier study, see C. James Schmidt, "Salary Plans for Academic Librarians ...," Protean, 2 (Summer, 1972) 22-25.

12. Cameron and Heim, 21.

13. The single exception to date (Claremont) will be explained in the following chapter.

Chapter 3

THE BARGAINING UNIT

When employees bargain collectively, they do so in clearly-defined units that remain stable through changing conditions in bargainable areas. Thus food-handlers do not make common cause with graduate assistants one year and then forsake them the next year to bargain in combination with typists.

Among faculty bargaining units recognized so far, few exclude librarians. Some of these, such as Lowell State and Saginaw Valley College, are mere curiosities, in the sense that they appear to have departed for no particular reason from the example of closely related institutions. Youngstown, bargaining in a state without a public employees' relations law, first excluded and later included librarians as part of the faculty unit. The "pure faculty" units at the University of Delaware and Fairleigh Dickinson furnish rare examples which may, however, portend important future differentiations in unit formation, as we shall see later in the chapter.

Of all the employees who are not universally accepted as faculty, librarians are most often included in faculty bargaining units. [1] Counselors of various kinds appear next most often, though they are excluded as often as not. Others appear sporadically in faculty units: non-supervisory

32

administrators, registrars, laboratory technicians, college physicians, coaches, laboratory-school teachers, editors, and archivists. In all faculty bargaining units, the classroom faculty are a majority; and in all, with the possible exception of SUNY, the faculty clearly dominate. Of course, we should remember that an exclusion of librarians from a faculty unit would not extend to library science teachers.

It is unlikely that the wording by which librarians are included with classroom faculty in a common unit is important to any but the most status-conscious. The official description of the unit often specifies librarians (e. g. , Adelphi, Boston State, Monmouth, Pennsylvania state colleges). It may, however, reflect an existing faculty status for librarians by not specifying them at all (e. g. , CUNY, Rhode Island College, and the University of Rhode Island). There is no point in building elaborately on these distinctions. The librarians of Oakland and of Central Michigan are faculty members, but are also specifically mentioned in the official unit descriptions. Administrations tend to seek, and unions to oppose, the exclusion of librarians, but the pattern is not universal. At Saginaw and Lowell, for instance, the union acquiesced in the exclusion of librarians, although under no legal obligation to do so. The AAUP at the University of Delaware and Fairleigh Dickinson did not include librarians. The administration of the University of San Francisco desired the inclusion of librarians and the union opposed it. At Florida Southern, the administration favored inclusion and the union adopted a neutral position. Some Wayne State faculty sought, but failed to get, a "pure" unit of classroom faculty only. [2]

Why would faculty unions desire to add librarians to their responsibility? One might think it tempting to win economic improvements for a homogeneous group such as classroom teachers and not have to share the fruits of bargaining; but there are countervailing considerations. Unions and administrations alike will be initially advised in part by their respective assessments of whether librarians would constitute a pro-union bloc in a certification election. Then, too, for a union a larger unit implies more bargaining power--at least until it becomes unwieldy; and, unwieldy or not, more members bring in more dues. [3]

These are reasons for an administration to oppose the inclusion of librarians. In addition, administrations have argued variously as follows. The measures of work, such as student credit-hour production, do not apply to librarians, who should not automatically receive the benefits of those whose work is measured. Then, again, the establishment of minimum salary levels for the unit may not require much outlay of money among the teaching faculty, but becomes disproportionately expensive when applied to librarians. Finally, practice regarding working conditions of librarians varies widely from university to university, here awarding and there withholding common faculty privileges such as rank, tenure, sabbaticals, and the academic work year. At the same time, the scope of agreements also varies, here describing and there ignoring these very privileges. Thus some reluctance to include librarians in a faculty unit stems from a fear that inclusion would in passing (almost accidentally) give them important new privileges which the administration, whether from economic motives or some local perceptions of their role, had not planned to accord.

In the earliest formations of faculty bargaining units, the inclusion of librarians was uneventful. The CUNY librarians bore enough of the traditional badges of faculty status to be included, in 1968, in the first formal faculty bargaining unit affecting four-year colleges. CUNY includes two-year colleges as well, and it should be remembered that among community colleges it has long been the rule to include librarians with classroom teachers in the bargaining unit. In 1969, however, the librarians of Central Michigan University were included in the faculty bargaining unit: the first such recognition in a purely four-year institution. Central Michigan librarians, quite coincidentally, enjoyed not only all of the usual signs of faculty status, but that less common mark, the academic work year. In Pennsylvania, some librarians of the state colleges enjoyed similar status and others did not. After minor dispute, librarians both with and without faculty rank were included in the faculty unit. [4] The librarians of Oakland were included in the faculty unit, even though they did not enjoy the academic work year. Thus in the earliest period of faculty unit determination, the inclusion of librarians occurred with a relative placidity inconsistent with the heated advocacy of faculty status appearing in library literature at the time. This placidity seems to have been the result of historical accident. If the earliest examples of faculty unit determination had occurred at institutions where librarians occupied a different place, they might well have been initially excluded, and the question of their being in a faculty unit would be a cause célèbre in library literature. In fact, they were not, and it is not.

Nevertheless, bargaining spread to institutions where librarians were less easily recognized as faculty members. Not surprisingly, however, another issue had arisen in the meantime, that had nothing to do with the faculty status of

librarians and yet much to do with how they would bargain.
In 1970 the NLRB considered the Cornell University case,
where one of several landmark issues was the desire of
UFCT to form and represent a unit comprising 17 professional and 20 non-professional library employees of the
Metropolitan District Office of the School of Industrial Relations.[5]   Joining in this triangular contest was the "Association of Cornell Employees--Libraries," seeking to form and
represent a unit of 270 non-professional library employees
throughout Cornell.   Thus the question of which librarians
were professional was not resolved, as NLRB dwelt on the
impropriety of fragmentation among campuses, and of the
separation of library non-professionals from other university
non-professional employees.

A crucial issue affecting academic librarians was resolved in the Long Island University (C. W. Post campus)
case in 1971.   This question was whether librarians should
be in a faculty unit.[6]   NLRB noted that although these librarians did not enjoy tenure or sabbatical leaves as the
faculty did, they had the following in common with faculty:
participation in faculty meetings; fringe benefits and salaries;
work with students; cooperation with other faculty members
in supplying books; and being listed as "with the rank" of
instructor or assistant professor.   They were thus included
in the unit.   On the Brooklyn campus of Long Island University (as NLRB had decided to treat the two campuses separately), it decided to include librarians in the unit, finding
that the professional librarians were professional employees
for reasons similar to those given in the C. W. Post case.
"They have all the benefits and privileges of faculty members of similar rank, including salary, except that none of
them is tenured and none receives sabbatical leave.   They

participate in faculty meetings. Although the Employer contends that the statutes do not permit them to vote, there is evidence that they have voted. They work 35 hours a week. In addition to performing the usual duties of librarians, they conduct sessions with students on effective use of the library. One of them has served on a thesis committee.... They also work with students individually, assisting them with library problems. Additionally, they work with faculty to be certain the library will be able to supply the books required by the courses given."

Fordham librarians did not have faculty status, but in 1971 NLRB included nonsupervisory professional librarians in a unit of faculty and "ancillary support professionals." The sole criterion stated in this decision was professionalism. [7]

The NLRB test at Florida Southern College in 1972 was more explicit and more reminiscent of C. W. Post: librarians voted at faculty meetings and made "substantial contributions to the education of students." In addition NLRB took note of the fact that they enjoyed tenure, though they had not done so at L. I. U. [8]

In 1971 a novel issue arose at Claremont when the Office and Professional Employees' International Union (AFL-CIO) sought a unit of professional librarians and other employees of the Honnold Library, which served the various corporate entities comprising Claremont Colleges. The complexities of this case led to some delay and referral to Washington NLRB. [9] It had its parallel, not in the cases involving whether librarians should be in faculty units, but rather in the Cornell case, which it resembled in several ways. There was a question of the library being an entity, and of whether a unit of professional and non-professional library employees constituted an appropriate unit. NLRB, having dealt with the problem of the library itself being an entity, approved a unit composed of all non-supervisory professional and non-professional library employees, even including student assistants who had worked over 600 hours. NLRB excluded as supervisors those who had supervision over bargaining unit members; and because this unit was so diverse a group, about half of the professional librarians were found to be supervisors and thus out of the unit. The professionals in the unit were left a minority. The tests which librarians had to pass to get into faculty or professional bargaining units do not apply in Claremont. This is no contradiction, but simply a result of the fact that for the only time since the Cornell case, NLRB had to consider how it would treat librarians when library employees and not the faculty sought to form a unit.

In deciding the appropriate unit at NYU in 1973, NLRB decided to include the librarians, but in this more complex environment felt called on to weigh differences against similarities. [10] The librarians, NLRB observed, differed at NYU from faculty in that: "Unlike faculty, the function of a librarian may change with title, and promotion may depend on the existence of a vacancy. Further distinguishing librarians from faculty are their regular workweek; retirement age; tenure requirements; separate grievance procedure; lack of proportional representation in the university senate (though the dean of libraries like other deans is a member); and, perhaps more basically, the fact that they are not considered faculty." Despite these distinctions (some of which are peculiar to NYU), librarians were included in the unit by NLRB, "as a closely allied professional group whose ultimate function, aiding and furthering the educational and scholarly goals of the University, converges with that of the faculty, though pursued through different means and in a different manner."

The Fordham law librarian was excluded in 1971, as a supervisor. Law librarians without law degrees were included in 1973 with the law faculty at the University of San Francisco, even though they taught no courses, because they met the NYU test above, and because the "relationship of the law librarians to the faculty is of critical importance in the supply and maintenance of this most essential research tool."[11]

These few examples suggest that as inclusion of librarians became accepted, ever easier standards of similarity to faculty sufficed. By now, at least with NLRB, professional status and converging goals are enough to unite librarians to a faculty unit. "Faculty status" is not essential to inclusion.

Some librarians are excluded from faculty units by NLRB because they are supervisory personnel. The NLRB definition of supervisors for this purpose appears to restrict the term to those who supervise other members of the bargaining unit in question, or who spend 50% or more of their time supervising employees who are not in that unit. Supervision itself is defined to require effective power to recommend the employment, reappointment, termination, and promotion of employees.

State-supported colleges and universities in states with public employee relations legislation fall under state rather than NLRB jurisdiction. It appears as if the states have generally followed NLRB on the inclusion of librarians in faculty units, though their definitions of supervisors and supervision may differ.

The faculty union has so dominated academic librarians' bargaining that we have few models to study for future and different developments. Claremont is a model, and need not be regarded as an aberration just because it is unique. It seems most likely that we shall see the growth of bargaining units of academic librarians, as distinct from faculty units. This growth could occur under any of three circumstances.

1) At some universities, the differences between the status, working conditions, and professional level of librarians and faculty may be so gross that the two groups would not have sufficient community of interest to form a single unit.

2) Faculty inaction or rejection of a bargaining agent leaves the librarians with the choice of going on with no agent, or waiting for the faculty to change its mind, or forming a unit that does not include faculty.

3) In the absence of a faculty unit, academic librarians may be scooped into some other bargaining unit in which they would form a minority. Such a unit could comprise counsellors, registrars, coaches, and similar support personnel who are found sometimes in, sometimes out of, present faculty units. Where academic librarians are public employees, they might conceivably find themselves in a unit of various public employees. NLRB is reluctant to mix professionals and non-professionals in the same unit,[12] but the Claremont example suggests that more depends on definitions of professionalism than on the pristine doctrine.

Superimpose on this functional classification of bargaining units their possible geographical arrangements, and we can see how simple has been our experience so far. We have seen that faculty units in a state system are sometimes local (as in Rhode Island and Massachusetts) and sometimes system-wide (as in Pennsylvania, New York, and New Jersey). Librarians with a common public employer (say a state board of regents) might form a system-wide unit, or be subsumed as a minority in a system-wide unit. The possibilities are extensive, the probabilities unknown.

The determination of bargaining units usually follows rules made by government agencies, which routinely deal with many and various employee groups. It thus occurs in a calm, only indirectly reflecting the interests that initiated the case, and devoid of the passions that attend a bargaining agent election. The unit determination nevertheless profoundly affects all of the subsequent bargaining relationship. It is critical to the aspirations of librarians. [13] Librarians in a faculty unit have usually shared in the non-economic provisions of the agreement. The librarians' evaluation procedures at Southeastern Massachusetts, and their grievance procedures at Temple, are among the few exceptions in which their treatment differs formally from that of the faculty. The economic position of librarians in faculty units forms a separate chapter. In all respects, however, the differences within a unit tend to be reduced. It should not be lost on librarians that niceties of "faculty status" have not been critical to their inclusion in the faculty bargaining unit. They are not even critical to the inclusion of classroom faculty in the unit.

A librarian's life in a non-faculty unit may prove quite different. The Claremont agreement, our only example at the four-year college level, affords no trace of faculty status or attributes to the librarians in the unit; and the whole relationship established by the unit determination accentuates the distinction between supervisor and unit member. Nor have faculty-type relationships characterized public librarians. [14] With limited experiences, we cannot speculate that an academic librarians' unit would achieve or even preserve to its members any characteristics of a faculty.[15]

Notes

1. Usually a description of the bargaining unit can be found in the "recognition clause" of the agreement, though occasionally this clause will merely cite a labor board decision instead. For the common inclusion of librarians in faculty units there is firm precedent in the schools. Donald Wollett and Robert Chanin, Law and Practice of Teacher Negotiations. Bureau of National Affairs, 1970. 2:28.

2. Robert L. Sawicki, "The Unionization of Professors at the University of Delaware," Liberal Education, 60 (Dec., 1974) 449-460; also William W. Boyer, "The Role of Department Chairmen in Collective Bargaining: The University of Delaware Experience," CUPA Journal 25 (April, 1974) 49-54. The Delaware unit was defined as all "regular members of the voting faculty." For the San Francisco contest, see 84 LRRM 1403; and for Florida Southern 80 LRRM 1160. The interest of some AAUP faculty at Wayne State in restricting the bargaining unit to classroom and research faculty is mentioned in J. David Kerr and Kenneth M. Smythe, "Collective Bargaining in Public Institutions," in Terrence N. Tice, ed., Faculty Power: Collective Bargaining on Campus. Institute for Continuing Legal Education, Ann Arbor, 1972. 368 pp., 54-56.

3. In Terrence Tice, ed., Faculty Power: Collective Bargaining on Campus. Institute for Continuing Legal Education, Ann Arbor, 1972, 368 pp., p. 151. William F. McHugh argues that the SUNY bargaining unit is not unwieldy.

4. G. Gregory Lozier and Kenneth P. Mortimer, Anatomy of a Collective Bargaining Election in Pennsylvania's

State-Owned Colleges. Center for the Study of Higher Education, Pennsylvania State University, 1974. 114 pp. 29-31.

5. 74 LRRM 1269.

6. 77 LRRM 1001 and 1006.

7. 78 LRRM 1177.

8. 80 LRRM 1160.

9. 81 LRRM 1317.

10. 83 LRRM 1549.

11. 84 LRRM 1403.

12. William F. McHugh, "Collective Bargaining with Professionals in Higher Education," Wisconsin Law Review, 55 (1971) no. 1, pp. 55-90; Wollett and Chanin, loc. cit.; and Russell A. Smith, Harry T. Edwards, and R. Theodore Clark, Labor Relations Law in the Public Sector. Bobbs Merrill, 1974. 1222 pp. 234-257.

13. Russell A. Smith, "Legal Principles of Public Sector Bargaining," in Tice, op. cit. , 12-13.

14. See, for example, "Collective Bargaining: Questions and Answers," ALA Bulletin, 62 (Dec. 1968) 1385-90.

15. As this goes to press, Brandeis University library clericals and non-supervisory librarians have formed a unit and engaged the Service Employees' International Union (AFL-CIO) as their agent.

Chapter 4

TERMS AND CONDITIONS OF EMPLOYMENT

"Wages, hours, and other terms and conditions of employment" is the time-worn description of what a bargaining agent is supposed to bargain. Not every term or condition is included in the description. Some matters are mandatory subjects of bargaining, some only permissive, and some even illegal. The scope varies with jurisdiction. The boundaries in academe are less clear than in industry, as there is less precedent so far to guide us, and much of university faculty work is unfamiliar not only in industry but in public schools. Some matters that faculty members consider an important part of their working conditions are discussed in the chapter on governance.

Certain interests of industrial labor have found little echo among faculty unions. Work shifts and work safety may be unique to the New Jersey state colleges agreement. A change in work shifts among librarians at Brooklyn College occasioned a grievance under a former CUNY agreement.

Tenure

The most important group of terms and conditions in academe can be classed as securities. Of these, the most basic is simply the assurance that one will remain among

44

the employed. From this rises the more complex question
of the meaning and practice of tenure. Where the institution of tenure conforms to AAUP standards (that is, most
colleges and universities), employment consists initially of
appointments for set terms, usually a year, with no assurance either that there will or will not be a reappointment.
The years preceding tenure need not be probationary, although a number of agreements refer to them as such, as
reappointment does not necessarily ensue upon satisfactory
performance. A satisfactory instructor might still not be
reappointed if the institution elects to have fewer employees,
or seeks a more promising occupant for the same position,
or moves the position from physics to chemistry so that
satisfactory performance is irrelevant. Reappointments follow a set number of years until tenure is granted. The
AAUP, long before it became a national union affiliation,
set a seven-year maximum for the pre-tenure period. [1]
Some universities are more "generous" than AAUP, in the
sense of having shorter pre-tenure periods, whether their
faculty are unionized or not. Some institutions with faculty
bargaining may bargain terms that fall short of AAUP
standards, as at Bloomfield College or (abortively) the University of Hawaii.

　　　Generally it is the aim of the NEA national affiliation
to reduce the probationary period to three years, to shift
onto the institution the burden of justifying non-renewal, and
to give the probationer an appeal to an outside arbitrator.
AFT also favors short probation and arbitration. [2]

　　　For the untenured, AAUP also sets minimum lengths
of notice of non-reappointment. These have been adopted
by most institutions, though here again changes either way
can be bargained. Three months' notice in the first year,

six in the second, and twelve in subsequent years are the AAUP standard.

When tenure is granted, it drastically alters the terms of employment. Tenure bestows procedural rights which shift the burden of proof from the faculty member to the employer in any question of terminating employment. The practical result is that there is hardly an employee with greater formal security than the tenured professor. Termination for incompetence is rare, and the hypothetical requirements for termination for moral turpitude are an exercise in bawdy speculation in faculty clubs. Termination as a result of retrenchment or financial exigency, though still relatively uncommon, is not taken lightly and will be treated separately.

The boundaries of tenure are more familiar in teaching departments, where it has a longer history, than in libraries. A professor of English has tenure as such, but not in his Dryden course. An assistant professor in the library has tenure as such, but not as a director or cataloger. [3]

Because tenure is such a good thing for its possessors, there has been little room for bargaining to embellish it on their behalf. It is therefore not a prominent feature in faculty agreements. There may be assurances that it will not be changed, as in the CUNY, SUNY, Temple, and Worcester agreements. Even where tenure is not mentioned at all, established practices would normally be protected from unilateral change by the existence of a formal bargaining relationship.

For the untenured, however, the institution of tenure may be a harsher condition than nothing at all. At the final crossroads of tenure or departure, the system permits no

compromise, no quiet gradual slipping into de facto security.
The untenured condition has therefore lent itself to a great
deal of collective bargaining. Criteria and eligibility for
tenure are described in such agreements as those at Monmouth, the Pennsylvania state colleges, Rhode Island College, St. John's, and Southeastern Massachusetts University.
Evaluation procedures may be included even if, as at CUNY,
they had already existed before collective bargaining. The
period before tenure could be longer than AAUP standards,
but, if bargained, is generally shorter. Unlike some institutions but still consistently with AAUP, the agreements at
Ferris, Southeastern Massachusetts, and the Pennsylvania
state colleges do not distinguish one academic rank from
another in establishing this pre-tenure period. Ferris,
Temple, and the Pennsylvania colleges refer to it as "probationary." Tenure significantly departed from AAUP
standards at Bloomfield College, where a tenure quota was
bargained and some faculty were placed in a category called
"tenure deferred due to ratio." Those in this class received
three-year appointments which might or might not be re-
newed. The New Jersey colleges agreement says nothing
about tenure because it is established by statute rather than
college policy.

It seems quite possible to bargain away tenure,
though there has been no conclusive court test so far. The
University of Hawaii and the American Federation of Teachers did just that in 1973, but the faculty refused to ratify
the pact and ousted the offending union. Tenure can be restricted at the bargaining table, as we have just seen in the
case of Monmouth. At Ferris it is restricted by an agency
shop agreement. Agency shop requires payment of a service fee to the union by all bargaining unit members, and

makes payment a condition of continued employment. The
union is not limited by the agreement in the fee it may set,
and tenure is no shelter for the professor who refuses to
pay. Agency shop may be statutory rather than bargained,
as in Rhode Island.

Librarians covered by faculty agreements usually enjoy the same tenure as their colleagues in the classroom.
The Pennsylvania colleges agreement extended tenure eligibility to junior librarians (classes I and II). There are
significant exceptions. At Southeastern Massachusetts University librarians were excluded from the peer evaluation
system by which faculty reappointments were to be considered. Their tenure is simply that after three years' service
they may be removed only for "just cause." Similarly,
Temple University librarians receive probationary appointments of one, one, and two years, and if then reappointed
for a fifth year they hold not traditional tenure but "regular
appointment." In SUNY, the decision not to reappoint a non-
tenured academic employee requires some degree of explanation; but if the decision was recommended by the peer
committee, that fact is the only explanation necessary.
Other reasons are required of a president who vetoes a
recommendation favoring the employee.

Academic Freedom

Tenure grew out of the need to safeguard academic
freedom, which is as essential to the entire university as
it is to the individual faculty member. It is thus not a
mere condition of employment, let alone a fringe benefit; but
it is only natural for the faculty, like AAUP, to regard it
as an essential part of the institution, and an individual's

right to security as well. [5]

Academic librarians, too, have claimed academic freedom in the ACRL/AAUP Joint Statement, which does not, however, clarify how it is to apply to librarians. [6] Presumably it means that, like other faculty members, librarians are free from censorship or reprisal for what they write and speak, though writing and speaking have not been as central a part of their work as of the classroom teachers'. What else may it mean? Book selection, perhaps, with the caveat that classroom faculty have some academic freedom in this area as well. A classroom teacher enjoys (if you can put it that way) the academic freedom to stop his survey of modern drama at 1930, or his biochemistry at 1960. Has a librarian an analogous freedom to continue classifying by Dewey after the library has switched to LC?

Collective bargaining has done little to clarify the application of academic freedom to librarians. The preamble of the CUNY agreement recognizes the applicability of academic freedom "to non-teaching members of the Instructional Staff, including counselors, to the extent their duties include research and publication of results, the selection of library or other educational materials or the formation of academic policy." The only clarification here is to limit the scope of the principle to certain specified areas, and these only if they are part of the librarian's duties.

Many agreements do not mention academic freedom-- no sign of course that it is not supported by both parties. Where it is mentioned, it is usually described in the language of AAUP's standards, whether AAUP or some other union is the agent at hand. This language does not expressly include or exclude librarians, and its application to them thus depends on the degree to which they have faculty status.

Retrenchment

Retrenchment, in the form of eliminating faculty or librarians' positions, is a new insecurity from which collective bargaining is seeking new protections. Tenure was not designed to prevent the university from abolishing a department or reducing the number of faculty in the face of financial pressure. The earliest faculty bargaining occurred when a renewal of depression experiences was still unimagined. Since then, such reductions have occurred among both tenured and non-tenured faculty, most noticeably at Antioch, Bloomfield, and Southern Illinois. [7] The anxieties created by such events soon appeared at bargaining tables as unions sought security from retrenchment. It is a rare union that can contract to prevent a university from reducing the number of its faculty, including those with tenure. Bard College is perhaps unique in having agreed to allow its union to decide whether a financial exigency requires a reduction of faculty. Unions can and do bargain for consultation on the question, for the manner in which eliminations are applied, and for their impact on the individual. At Wayne State University, therefore, the problem is treated as one of "layoff and recall." The agreement establishes an order of priority in releasing members of the bargaining unit. Subject to the needs of the academic program, layoffs must be effected first among the non-tenured, and within this group in order of seniority ("last in, first out"). Then if further retrenchment is still necessary the tenured faculty are to be laid off in the same fashion. All are to be given suitable opportunities for employment within the university.

Within two years, if positions are restored, those qualified for them are to be recalled in inverse order ("last out, first in"). The Pennsylvania state colleges have a similar system for layoff but not for recall. Seniority is modified by a requirement that whatever faculty are left must have the "necessary qualifications to teach the remaining courses." At Southeastern Massachusetts University, retrenchment is to be carried out in order of seniority "except in the most unusual circumstances," and for the next five years those retrenched have a right to be rehired for any position for which they are qualified.

Temple has a separate retrenchment provision for librarians, based on seniority but also subject to library operational needs. Otherwise, there is little specific provision for retrenching librarians. Where there is none the question depends on their local status as faculty. The fact that nobody intended a provision to have a certain effect does not prevent its having that effect, and agreements can spring surprises on all. Librarians should therefore ask themselves questions along the following lines: At institutions where librarians do not have full tenure rights and the agreement calls for retrenchment of non-tenured bargaining unit members before those who are tenured, what would be the effect on librarians in case of extensive retrenchment? At institutions where recall is by seniority and qualification, might an English professor with high seniority occupy a literature bibliographer's position instead of its former occupant who had lower seniority? Can the special efforts and procedures that have been undertaken in order to carry out affirmative action regarding the employment of women and minorities be undone by a seniority system of layoff and recall?

Promotion

Security means more than the ability to cling to a
position. Academics pursue a career, and hold certain
hopes and expectations in their profession. Most of them
would probably not have chosen to endure years at one level
had they not had some calculable hope of achieving a higher
level, whether by creativity, diligence, or mere seniority.
Among the faculty, reaching a higher level consists ordin-
arily of promotion in rank. The career goal of perhaps
most instructors is to become a professor. Those en
route in this system do not like new criteria to make
achievement of their goal more difficult, and thence flows
a belief that promotion opportunity is not only a working
condition but one in which the individual is entitled to security. This kind of security is sought through systems where-
by promotion occurs automatically upon the fulfillment of
certain specified and concrete minimum requirements.

The New Jersey state colleges list minimum requirements for each rank. Pennsylvania colleges set procedures
and criteria additional to the minimum set by Pennsylvania
statute. CUNY states promotion goals (30% professors,
30% associates, 30% assistants, and 10% instructors) for
the whole faculty. [8] Central Michigan sets a time-table
for recommendations for promotion. The Oakland agreement
mentions promotion only as a management right.

Among librarians the picture is more obscure.
Criteria for academic promotion usually include doctorates,
research, publication, and teaching effectiveness. [9] The last
is hard for librarians to demonstrate, and the rest are
relatively rare among them, outside of the library schools.
Few librarians therefore break the barrier between

assistant and associate professor. Their dilemma is that this very frustration has seemed to result from their being treated as faculty: to partake fully of faculty promotions requires their arguing that they are after all different from faculty, and should get their prizes by playing under different (others would say easier) rules. Not so, say a few librarians more recently: the problem is that librarians are not treated completely like faculty: give us their summers and we can meet the same criteria. This point will be discussed below, with the librarians' work year.

Librarians have another route to advancement (professional rather than academic) within the administrative structure of the library. Ability can sometimes be rewarded in this way even where academic promotion criteria are procrustean.

There is, finally, a familiar bastard system in which academic rank is given according to the level of administrative responsibility. ACRL opposes this practice in its Statement, probably because the principle is different from that governing the classroom faculty, and in their eyes cheapens the coinage. Administrative work can both require and develop a high degree of learning and professionalism, and it would be parochial to ignore the fact in assessing eligibility for promotion. On the other hand, librarians with no administrative interest or aptitude can also develop a high degree of learning and professionalism, and it is unfair to deny them recognition solely on the basis of their place in a hierarchy.

Few faculty agreements make any special accommodation to librarians' promotions. Silence has different meanings according to the history of the institution. At Ferris and SUNY, it leaves librarians unequal, as they were before.

At Central Michigan, Oakland, Rhode Island College, Rutgers, and the University of Rhode Island, silence implies the same criteria for promotion of librarians as for other faculty. Southeastern Massachusetts and some of the Massachusetts colleges make a small formal adjustment for librarians by specifying "professional" rather than "classroom" effectiveness as a criterion for promotion. The Temple agreement is most explicit regarding promotion for librarians, specifying procedures, appeals, and some of the criteria. It provides for the library faculty to establish criteria with the consent of the director, but in addition it sets up criteria within the agreement: "1) effectiveness of performance as a librarian; 2) evidence of continuing professional growth; 3) effectiveness of service to the library; 4) scholarly performance; 5) years of service in rank." Librarians are treated separately in the agreement because of differences from other faculty criteria, and because promotion for the rest of Temple faculty has ample roots in existing practice. Librarians are distinguished by Temple not only from faculty but from "academic professionals," for whom there is yet another career track.

Workload

Workload is familiar enough in industry and in the public schools. The term has crept into public higher education more recently. [10] It is so difficult to measure what a professor does that program-budget devotees have identified that part of the whole that seems measurable, and called it Workload. Thus Professor A works with fifteen students, imparting to them the unique process and product of ten years' investigation which he had to know three languages just to conduct; and he produces 45 student credit hours. Professor B teaches his economics out of <u>Newsweek</u> to thirty students, and their outside reading consists of being sent to <u>Newsweek</u> to verify the correctness of the lectures; and he produces 90 student credit hours. That is workload at work. Librarians are less often measured in this way, perhaps because they cost so much less.

The SPA/CUNY standing library committee in 1972 made a presentation to the union bargaining team. The librarians' proposals included such workload elements as the reduction of their work week from 35 to 30 hours a week, and staffing with library technical assistants to help offset a workload that (in public services) had gone from 1300 students per librarian in 1969 to 1800:1 in 1972. Although the union included these proposals, they did not survive bargaining and the final agreement did not change the librarians' workload.

The Oakland AAUP in 1973 included the following among its proposals:

> The library faculty who do not teach credit-delivering courses are not part of the present student/faculty ratio. They are the only group of faculty in the bargaining unit not covered by this constraint on work-load. The AAUP proposes to close the gap by a student/bargaining unit librarian ratio of 520:1.

The AAUP explained that the ratio had deteriorated from 328:1 in 1966-67 to a projected 521:1 in 1973-74. This proposal, too, did not survive bargaining.

For librarians in general, bargaining has either declined to describe workload altogether or expresses it as a certain number of hours' work per week. Even though this kind of clause immediately sets librarians apart from classroom faculty, it may in some libraries represent an improvement in working conditions.

Work-Year

Of greater importance to academic librarians is the span of their contractual year. [11] Historically, institutions that were formerly normal schools or teachers' colleges tended to have nine-month contracts for librarians as well as teachers. Following their conversion to broader roles, many of these colleges have been establishing year-round duty for librarians, usually about eleven months. For this change there are two interrelated arguments. The first argument is economic, suggesting that it is disadvantageous to the institution to pay existing salaries to librarians for only nine months' service. The second argument is that library service to the university requires the presence of the librarians throughout the year: there are students all summer; and, even more conclusive, books come in all year and need to be handled.

The first argument is valid only if the librarians are to be paid less for each added month than they are being paid for each of the basic nine months. To pay less is a simple, straightforward reduction in the rate of compensation. One might think that if the institution has the desire and the power to accomplish this end, it can do so more frontally and not have to rely on a stratagem like tinkering with the calendar. If, however, librarians desire to increase their annual income even at diminishing rates of return, then institution and librarians are well on their way to collusion. Not infrequently, the reaction of outside librarians to the Central Michigan librarians' academic year contract is to ask what are the chances of working through the summer.

The second argument, as to the need for library service all year, depends partly on the summer programs of the institution and partly on the division of labor that prevails within the library. Enrollments in the summer tend to be only a third or fourth of the regular terms. There may therefore be an economy for the institution in not fully staffing public services during the summer. Then too, if the summer enrollment consists largely of schoolteachers qualifying for salary raises by molding puppets and memorizing class notes, it is an extravagance to require a full complement of librarians to witness the spectacle.

So much for the interests of the institution. Librarians have shown varying interests. Some would sell their summers for cash if they could. Others argue the inequity of requiring them to meet normal faculty standards for promotion while denying them the opportunity, so freely accorded to classroom teachers, to meet the standards. If Virgil Massman's findings are widely applicable, this argument fails, for his survey of a few midwestern states reveals that academic librarians with nine-month contracts have published slightly less per capita than those on year-round contracts.[12] The results, however, are affected by an obvious selective factor, which is that less bibliographic and subject-matter research probably occurs in the former teachers' colleges than in the older universities.

The arguments of librarians in favor of the shorter year appear to have been that it would benefit them specifically in gaining promotion; and that it is essential to their status as faculty. There appears to be no published effort to persuade university administrators, or even faculty, of its benefit to the institution.

To some extent this failure explains why at the bargaining table the academic calendar for librarians has remained a minor issue despite sporadic progress. The university side is allowed to think that the change would be costlier than it probably really needs to be, that vital services would lapse, and that there is little institutional need for a library staff that indulges in scholarship. The union side is allowed to share these views, and to believe that the cost of the librarians' calendar change would significantly compete with their general salary demands. Librarians themselves are a major source of ambivalence regarding the question of their calendar, as many are simply not sure whether they want summers free, or would try to trade them for dollars if they got them. Little wonder, then, that the merits of the academic calendar have been obfuscated, that the ACRL Statement merely formalizes this confusion, and that collective bargaining has so far reflected it. It is difficult for the union to support the position with confidence when, as at Wayne State University, it was unclear whether the primary goal was free summers or added compensation for summers. The academic year was supported both by LACUNY and by the chief librarians of CUNY, but did not survive the bargaining table. [13]

New Jersey state college librarians were given the individual option, through bargaining, of converting from a full to an academic year (if agreeable locally), at a pro-rata reduction in salary. A similar provision at Temple makes the librarian's seniority an added criterion which can, however, be overriden in favor of someone whose previous year's request failed. At Adelphi, collective bargaining gained a partial but significant improvement in the librarians'

calendar. Formerly, the librarians had had an eleven-
month contract, and they now gained a ten-month contract.
The rest of the faculty teach nine months a year.

The librarians' proposals to the union bargaining
team at CUNY in 1972 included an academic year appointment, though with staggered annual leaves. This too failed
in bargaining, as the result of a fact-finder's recommendation against "placing librarians on academic calendars."

At Oakland in 1973 an interesting story began with the
following union proposal:

> The AAUP proposes that professional librarians in
> the bargaining unit be given academic year appoint-
> ments.
>
> Librarians on academic year appointments would
> work two regular semesters or one regular sem-
> ester plus Spring and Summer terms. The
> scheduling will be done with the consultation of the
> Dean of the Library, the Dean of the summer
> school, and the individual library faculty members
> involved. Librarians presently work eleven months
> with one month vacation. The extra time is needed
> by librarians for professional growth. It is ex-
> pected that the time will be used for further study,
> research, and course planning.
>
> The cost of this change in appointment will be zero
> in terms of librarians' salaries....
>
> Librarians have always taught students on a one-
> to-one basis in small, informal groups. The trend
> now is to more formal classroom teaching of li-
> brary skills and subject bibliography in addition....
>
> The AAUP submits that the time to complete the
> implementation of librarians' faculty status by giv-
> ing them academic year appointments is long
> overdue....

The demand was heavily documented, citing among others
the ACRL-AAUP Joint Statement and J. Carlyle Parker's

"Faculty Status and the Academic Work Year. "[14]

In the manner of bargaining, the two sides approached until at last the only differences between them were: 1) whether six or only five professional development leaves should be available each year to the librarians; 2) whether these leaves should be for a semester at full pay or (as the University proposed) a choice of two months at full pay or four at half pay; and 3) whether librarians were entitled to all the holidays and academic recesses provided the faculty in the faculty handbook. As the parties had agreed to submit to arbitration matters on which they could not reach agreement, these final offers were arbitrated. The arbitrator, taking into consideration what he called "the underlying thrust of the Association's original proposal, to make the working conditions of the faculty of the library more equal to the rest of the faculty, and the University's willingness to compromise to a reasonable degree with this effort," chose the AAUP position in all three differences. [15]

Bargaining is thus a way of pursuing calendar reform for librarians. If these efforts have not been widely successful it is not the process that is to blame, but the failure to persuade both the union and the administration of whatever virtues the calendar reform possesses.

As usual, bargaining relationships protect existing calendars. Where the academic year survives for librarians, it would probably be impossible to change it without bargaining. Moreover, the austere self-examination required by bargaining may eventually eliminate the muddling that both sides have indulged in on this subject.

Other Working Conditions

The tradition of sabbatical leaves is one of the

hallmarks of faculty status. For our purposes, they are much like promotions, in that the eligibility of librarians depends on practice before bargaining. Sabbaticals are mentioned in such agreements as those at Ferris, Rhode Island College, St. John's, Southeastern Massachusetts, the University of Rhode Island, and Boston State, with no provision either to include or exclude librarians. Many, such as Oakland, Worcester, CUNY, SUNY, and Central Michigan, have not found it necessary to describe their sabbatical policies in their agreements. The Pennsylvania state colleges agreement specifically made librarians eligible for sabbaticals, dating their eligibility in each case from their acquisition of faculty rank.

Research funds have not loomed large in agreements. At Central Michigan, funds that might otherwise have been devoted to merit bonuses were distributed for meritorious research and teaching projects. Librarians are equally eligible for these funds.

The achievement of certain faculty working conditions preceded or occurred independently of faculty collective bargaining. For example, CUNY librarians in 1965 became eligible for all faculty perquisites except the academic work-year.[16] Sabbaticals and tenure were accorded University of Kentucky librarians in 1966,[17] nine-month appointments at Alfred in 1968,[18] and sabbaticals and tenure at Pennsylvania State University in 1969.[19] By 1969 at least two of the New Jersey and three of the Pennsylvania state colleges reported equivalency to faculty in titles, promotion criteria, sabbaticals, and participation in governance.[20]

It is impossible to list all of the working conditions of librarians. One clause in the CUNY agreement exempts certain librarians from guard duty, and thereby suggests

that bargained agreements are the top of the iceberg and
little-known practices are the bulk of it. From library to
library, time is handled rigidly or loosely: coffee breaks
and the length of the work week are defined or not, to the
comfort or distress of those who place a high value on cer-
tainty. Librarians may be required to work at night and on
week-ends. Some like and some resent wearing name-tags,
sharing the staff lounge with outside faculty visitors, or giving written reports of conventions that they have attended at
library expense. Faculty lounges, parking, air conditioning,
parental leave, and day-care centers have also appeared at
least as demands. [21] These and many more are conditions
of employment, and most are proper subjects for collective
bargaining if the need arises.

Notes

1. "Academic Freedom and Tenure, Statement of Princi-
    ples, 1940," AAUP Bulletin, 27 (Feb. 1941) 40-45.
    Also, "1968 Recommended Institutional Regulations
    on Academic Freedom and Tenure," AAUP Bulletin,
    54 (Winter 1968) 448-452.

2. Virginia Lee Lussier, "National Faculty Associations
    in Collective Bargaining: A Comparative Discus-
    sion," ACBIS Special Report No. 8 (June 1974) 21
    pp.

3. Commission on Academic Tenure in Higher Education.
    Faculty Tenure. Jossey-Bass, 1973. 276 pp.
    Also, William Van Alstyne, "Tenure and Collective
    Bargaining," Current Issues in Higher Education,
    26 (1971) 210-217.

4. Chronicle of Higher Education, 8 (Nov. 26, 1973) 1.

5. George Louis Joughin, Academic Freedom and Tenure.
    U. of Wisconsin, 1967. 343 pp. 324.

6. "Joint Statement on Faculty Status of College and

University Librarians," College and Research Libraries News (Sept. 1973) 209-212.

7. Chronicle of Higher Education, 8 (June 28, 1974) 3.

8. "Position Paper Submitted to and Approved by the Negotiating Committee of the Legislative Conference of the College of the City of New York on March 2, 1972," LACUNY Journal, 1 (Spring, 1972) 29-30. Thomas Atkins, the signatory for LACUNY, pointed out at that time that the actual rank distribution for CUNY librarians was 5, 13, 40, 42.

9. Carl Hintz, "Criteria for Appointment to and Promotion in Academic Rank," College and Research Libraries, 29 (Sept. 1968) 341-346. Also, "Model Statement of Criteria and Procedures for Appointment, Promotion in Academic Rank, and Tenure for College and University Librarians," College and Research Libraries News, (Sept. 1973) 192-195.

10. "Statement on Faculty Workload," AAUP Bulletin, 52 (Winter, 1966) 385-386.

11. J. Carlyle Parker, "Faculty Status and the Academic Work Year," California Librarian, 33 (July, 1972) 143-149. Also, Harry R. Gates, "The Academic Status Illusion and the Nine-month Contract," PNLA Quarterly, 36 (Winter, 1972) 3-6.

12. Virgil F. Massman, Faculty Status for Librarians. Scarecrow, 1972. 229 pp.

13. See footnote 8, 2nd: Council of Chief Librarians (CUNY), "Recommendations Regarding New Contract for Instructional Staffs," LACUNY Journal, 1 (Winter, 1972) 35.

14. California Librarian, 33 (July, 1972) 143-149.

15. In the Matter of Arbitration between Oakland University ... and American Association of University Professors... (August, 1973). Processed. 12 pp.

16. Wilson Library Bulletin (January, 1966) 407. Also, Library Journal, 91 (June 15, 1966) 219-220.

17. *Library Journal*, 91 (June 15, 1966) 3160.

18. *Library Journal*, 93 (Nov. 1, 1968) 4086.

19. *Library Journal*, 94 (Jan. 1, 1969) 20.

20. "Librarians and Faculty Status," *College and Research Libraries News*, 30 (March, 1969) 1.

21. *Chronicle of Higher Education*, 8 (Nov. 26, 1973) 14.

Chapter 5

GOVERNANCE BARGAINED

The farther librarians have been from faculty status,
the more vaguely have they described it.   Until 1970 it appeared (at least in library literature) as a collection of
fringe benefits.   Then David Kaser showed that equality
with the faculty necessarily included the traditional faculty
roles in governance,[1] and M. P. Marchant published his
study of participation for librarians as a mode of management.[2]   The pursuit, which may have begun as an uncritical
emulation of the faculty, has brought more knowledge of the
object of the chase.   The chief casualty of this knowledge
is the simplicity of the cause.   A goal which may once
have consisted merely of titles, faculty club, and Blue
Cross has been eclipsed by Kaser's model of familiar faculty governance and by Marchant's model of participation
techniques taken from non-academic areas.   Other models
now loom as well: extensions of faculty roles independently
of collective bargaining, traditional employee powers under
collective bargaining, and the aspirations, claims, and
achievements of faculty unions.   "Participatory management"
may be less or greater than the familiar academic governance roles of the faculty.   Beverly Lynch has most usefully
mustered the favorable and unfavorable arguments regarding
it.[3]   Though each deserves attention, our purpose suggests

comparing faculty governance powers with those which collective bargaining holds out, and then considering how academic librarians partake of each.

Traditional Faculty Governance

A joint statement by the American Association of University Professors, the American Council on Education, and the Association of Governing Boards of Universities and Colleges describes the traditional place of faculty in governance in part as follows"

> The faculty has primary responsibility for such fundamental areas as curriculum, subject matter and methods of instruction, research, faculty status, and those aspects of student life which relate to the educational process....
>
> Faculty status and related matters are primarily a faculty responsibility; this area includes appointments, decisions not to reappoint, promotions, the granting of tenure, and dismissal....
>
> The governing board and president should, on questions of faculty status, as in other matters where the faculty has primary responsibility, concur with the faculty judgment except in rare instances and for compelling reasons which should be stated in detail.
>
> The faculty should actively participate in the determination of policies and procedures governing salary increases.
>
> The chairman or head of a department, who serves as the chief representative of his department within an institution, should be selected either by departmental election or by appointment following consultation with members of the department and of related departments: appointments should normally be in conformity with department members' judgment.... [4]

An AAUP survey of 970 institutions (about 800 of them four-year) showed that in 1969-70 decisions which Garbarino classifies as "personnel" were either determined by the faculty or required their joint action in 25% of the institutions, and that formal consultation with the faculty occurred in another 27%. These "personnel matters," however, include general and individual salary determinations, in which faculty participation is rare. In 34% of the institutions tenure was determined by the faculty or required their joint action, while formal consultation with the faculty occurred in another 29%. Other aspects of governance were classified as "academic" and "administrative." Faculty participation involved either determination or joint action in 67% of the institutions in "academic matters"; and in "administrative matters," 21%.

Thus hiring, retention, tenure, and promotion rest primarily in the hands of academic colleagues. Traditionally, too, the faculty have a strong though not final voice in the selection of department heads or chairmen, and, to diminishing degrees, of deans, provosts, and presidents. So broad a description is necessarily affected by local variables such as the history and level of the institution, the style and quality of its administrators, the intellectual level of its faculty, and the political and fiscal environment of the institution.

As Seymour Lipset writes, "... most of the malpractices occur in state teachers colleges and other less academylike institutions. With some exceptions, the lower the status of a college in academe, the more arbitrary is its president's power."[5] If we are to judge from AAUP investigations and reports, open violations of traditional faculty rights are relatively infrequent.

The traditional powers of the faculty seem less impressive when faculty positions are being eliminated. Not only this financial shrinkage but student self-assertion, central state bureaucracies, and the professionalization of administration have brought new fears to the faculty.

Unions and Participation

Since a bargained agreement is itself a "joint decision," it can be argued that an agreement that does not change existing tenure policy, or provide for "discussion" with faculty before retrenchment, represents a joint decision as to how to handle these issues. Proponents of faculty collective bargaining argue from a premise that to bargain governance expands the faculty role in it.[6] Not the most bashful in presenting this view are the major faculty unions. Belle Zeller, president of the CUNY union, ascribes several advantages to collective bargaining. Those related to governance are: political power, a faculty role in establishing budget priorities, shared responsibility and accountability for both faculty and administrators, and resistance to outside pressures.[7] Alfred Sumberg of AAUP regards governance as an integral part of faculty negotiations, declaring that "it does not follow that the academic community must pattern its organization after industrial unions. Public school teachers who organized in the 1960s made this fundamental error and have had to live with the consequences.... Faculties should regard collective bargaining as a means of putting into effect the goals of the past fifty years."[8]

A National Education Association official writes: "Nothing has affected the role and status of the college professor more than the emergence, within these vast

organizations, of a new managerial class that exists solely
to keep the organization machine running. This new class
has gradually arrogated to itself all the real decision-making
powers.... Thus, collective bargaining provides the basis
for the first really effective instrument of faculty power and
participation in the decision-making process, because for
the first time, faculty is able--through its bargaining agent
at the bargaining table--to come to grips with the real decision-making authority of the university. "[9]

Non-union observers, and of course administrators,
have been less sanguine. A college president with a background in labor law wrote, "If a faculty is unionized, I believe the result will be an exclusion of faculty from areas
of governance, rather than a continuation or expansion. "[10]
The New York Times, in an editorial during CUNY negotiations, expressed anxiety as to "whether decisions concerning faculty tenure will continue to remain in the hands of
the academic departments or increasingly be turned over to
union grievance committees and outside arbitrators. "[11]
Garbarino in 1971 and Coleman in 1972 noted that collective
bargaining was undermining senates. [12] James Begin in
1974 questioned this conflict, but largely at the price of
supposing that the Massachusetts state college agreements
did not dismantle faculty governance. An independent poll
of faculty and administrators in six SUNY institutions (which,
however, included community colleges) showed a strong belief that collective bargaining had increased faculty participation in decision-making there. [13] Garbarino and Aussieker
summarized the effect of unions on governance in 1975 as
follows:

> In some institutions with undeveloped systems of
> faculty participation they have succeeded in

> increasing the influence of faculty in institutional
> decision-making. They have not expanded the
> area of decisions in which faculty participate be-
> yond those that have been traditional to the gov-
> ernance systems of major universities, but they
> have raised more institutions to that level of par-
> ticipation.... Although, to date, the effect of un-
> ions on academic senates does not seem to have
> been major, in the long run the net effect is likely
> to be a diminution in the role of the senates as
> there is a reduction in the range and importance
> of matters left to senate procedure. [14]

Events, too, have shown some conflict between collective bargaining and faculty governance. At the University
of Hawaii, AFT and the University initialled an agreement
that would have bargained away tenure but for a vote by
which the faculty refused to ratify the agreement that its
agent had made on its behalf. [15] In Pennsylvania, the SUPA
union lodged a suit to abolish the Pennsylvania State University senate on the grounds that it was a company union. [16]
At Central Michigan, an academic senate resolution declaring teaching effectiveness to be one of the criteria for promotion, and student opinion an element in its evaluation,
occasioned an unfair-labor-practice suit by the faculty union
against the university. [17]

No consideration of the relation of collective bargaining to faculty governance can ignore the exceptional power
of the bargaining table in any matter on which the two sides
agree. Decisions at the table can substantially constrict
areas of faculty judgment by modifying or abolishing tenure,
or by making tenure readily available to all, or by nullifying
the financial importance of academic promotion. Student
powers can be reduced or extended. The bargaining agent
is just that--an agent, empowered to act for the entire bargaining unit. The duty of the agent is to optimize the wages,

hours, and other working conditions of its constituency. Whether a different relation is possible remains to be seen. In the meantime, it is not the union's duty to accept what Garbarino calls "the primacy of academic concerns," which he found to characterize senates. The agreement that the union makes with the employer is not everything that either desires. It is the result of bartering between the two. There are several major trading items at the table: governance, security, union power, and not least of all, money. A union can sincerely agree to seek some special interest among its constituency, and still do its duty by trading off some such items to get others. [18]

There is another enemy to faculty participation: geographical centralization of authority. This process has occurred in many states, sometimes resulting in the state college systems that we have been citing in New Jersey, New York, Massachusetts, Pennsylvania, Rhode Island, and so on. Centralized systems are based on the premise that institutions funded from the same source should generally not compete with each other nor duplicate each other's programs unnecessarily, and that there are economies of scale to be achieved by budgeting a whole system instead of a miscellany. Opponents question whether these advantages outweigh those of local autonomy: flexibility, enterprise, sensitivity to local situations, esprit de corps, and the recognition of variety for its own sake rather than as a necessary evil. These balances of conflicting values are not new, but educational costs, program budget methods, and financial stringency have given centralization political allure.

Now collective bargaining adds to the attractiveness of centralization in more than one interest group. The existing aversion of state budget bureaus to competition among their institutions of higher education can only be heightened if they detect whipsawing. A high settlement with the union at university A becomes the minimum settlement acceptable to the union at university B, whether the unions have the same or rival affiliations. Even more ominous, the various unions may show signs of consolidation. Statewide management then intervenes to resolve these threats by centralizing bargaining. If the pressure for centralization is fiscal, the emphasis on centralized bargaining is likely to be overwhelmingly fiscal. The impact of this attitude of governance is plain. [19]

To see effects of collective bargaining on academic governance we must depend on actual experience evidenced by agreements, rather than the published speculations of enthusiasts. The following cases are arranged to show a spectrum ranging from the specific and radical reorganizations in Massachusetts to the subtle commingling of bargaining with long-established relationships at Rutgers.

The greatest formal change in governance to be accomplished through collective bargaining has occurred in those colleges of the Massachusetts state college system that engage in collective bargaining, for example Boston State College and Worcester State College. As its architect writes, the proposal originated with the central administration. [20] Typically, the main governing body is a tripartite council comprising administration, faculty, and student representatives; and similarly-constituted committees deal with curriculum, admissions, calendar, student life, and so on. It could be argued that the council is quadripartite, as the union president and vice president are expressly accorded seats, and the faculty (whether they pay union dues or not) elect other representatives. Students are excluded from certain areas in which the union and the administration agreed that faculty had a "special and dominant interest": evaluation of faculty members for tenure and promotion; workload; and faculty grievance procedures. Thus, in crude numerical terms, the faculty have half the voice in decisions on reappointment, evaluation, tenure, promotion, and grievances; and a third or fourth of the voice on other matters traditionally associated with faculty governance.

The agreement between St. John's University and the AAUP, after long struggle, is probably as broad in its treatment of university governance as the Massachusetts examples, though far different in approach. The whole AAUP Statement on Government is incorporated by reference into the agreement, with the result that anybody who believes that the terms of the Statement are not being followed properly can allege a contract violation in grievance. Elected search committees nominate candidates for deans' positions, and whoever is chosen must have the approval of the committee. A tripartite committee of administrators, students, and union representatives advises on the academic calendar. The academic senate continues, but is not represented on such committees and cannot handle any matters taken care of by the agreement. Appointments, tenure, and promotions are recommended by the departments, and the administration must give written reasons for not accepting these recommendations.

The New Jersey state college system has bargained, first with the New Jersey Education Association and later with the New Jersey Federation of Teachers, important changes in governance. These are not as formally radical as the Massachusetts examples nor as vigorous an entrenchment of familiar faculty roles as that at St. John's.

Department chairmen are elected by the department faculty, subject to a veto by the college president with written or oral reasons. Other personnel decisions are simply covered by a provision in the agreement that departments must follow their own procedures consistently in making reappointment and promotion recommendations. Potentially the most far-reaching feature of the New Jersey agreement, however, is its provision for direct union representation on every college-wide committee and every system-wide advisory committee in which bargaining unit members are included. The union may also speak at trustees' meeting.

The four-year colleges of the City University of New York had a well-defined structure of academic decision-making before collective bargaining, and the faculty controlled educational policy and personnel recommendations at the department level. [21] The bargained agreement thus builds on existing machinery, the basic particle of which is the departmental personnel and budget committee. Academic matters are not directly treated in the agreement, except for provisions establishing the academic work year and a goal for the proportion of each academic rank in the faculty. Evaluation is largely in the hands of the departmental personnel and budget committees, with certain added procedures required by the agreement. Both the agreement and university policies are grievable, and can culminate in binding arbitration. Chapter 6, on Contract Administration, explains the effects of this arbitration more fully.

Central Michigan University, the first after CUNY to have collective bargaining with its faculty, has also pioneered in what Neil Bucklew calls "employment negotiation." [22] The object here is to use the agreement for customary union concerns while relying in academic matters on processes

already developed. Departments that had not developed such
procedures were required by a former agreement to do so
in 1972, but no particular kind of procedures was dictated to
them. Other elements of faculty governance continue as before, particularly the senate and its committee structure.
The 1974-77 agreement introduced binding arbitration in
strictly contract grievances and in cases where the president
might veto the reappointment recommendation of a senate
hearing committee (the highest appeal stage under faculty
control). The president is to give "compelling reasons" for
such a veto (AAUP language and CMU policy before bargaining arrived). The arbitrator's sole task is to determine
whether the president's reasons are compelling. The union
(a Michigan Education Association affiliate) has indicated dis-
satisfaction with the theory of employment negotiations.

Rutgers, with a long tradition of AAUP leadership
and a vigorous senate, has a collective bargaining agreement
with AAUP that may well deal less concretely with academic
matters than any other faculty agreement. If financial exi-
gencies lead the university to terminate an academic program
or a number of faculty members, or to suspend promotions,
then the problem is to be referred to a joint AAUP-Rutgers
committee for evaluation. That appears to be the only direct
reference to academic policy in the agreement. Grievances
at Rutgers may be based either on the agreement or on university regulations and procedures regarding tenure and promotion. Grievances end with the university, rather than an
arbitrator. The agreement declares that the grievance
process is not to diminish anyone's responsibility for exercising academic judgment. This informality in no way de-
notes a weak union, but stems rather from the close relations that existed between the senate and the AAUP before

collective bargaining and that have continued since. In 1974, however, the AAUP demanded, among other matters: 1) the right to appoint three bargaining unit members as voting members to the board of governors and the board of trustees; 2) the right to participate in the selection, evaluation, terms of appointment, and dismissal of university administrators; 3) the right to a role in forming the university budget in areas that impact on terms and conditions of employment; and 4) union representation on governance committees. The New Jersey Public Employment Relations Commission decided against AAUP. [23]

The effect of bargaining is not restricted to the direct treatment of matter. The blandest agreement can effect a devolution of power and responsibility if its grievance provisions permit. By definition, an appeals system extends outside the circle of colleagues who made the original decision, and outside the department where the expertise is presumed to reside. Appeals systems in and out of bargaining carry the question further and further from this center of expertise, and from peer evaluation. Under collective bargaining, they often carry the question outside of the institution, to a state education board or employee relations commission, or to a professional arbitrator with or without a background in university life. Where appeals call substantive judgments into question, the derogation from peer evaluation, and consequently from faculty power, is great. Even appeals restricted apparently to procedural error are inhibiting to the exercise of a professional or academic judgment.

The simple righteousness of being in favor of "due process" can mask power struggles in which the grievance machinery is a major union weapon. Some (not all) unions, for instance, would prefer to shorten probationary periods and spread the privileges of tenure as widely as possible among members of the bargaining unit. If they cannot accomplish this end at the bargaining table, they can pursue it by supporting grievances based on the same assumption. Grievances will be discussed further when we discuss administering the agreement.

To go now from academe in general to its librarians in particular, the few perceptions of librarians so far vary widely. Kaser attributed the advent of collective bargaining in academic libraries to the absence of a participative structure. [24] Holley considered that a desire for greater participation is founded simply in the belief that it will bring greater benefits. [25] De Gennaro regarded the conservatism of unions as inimical to the development of participation. [26]

The participation of academic librarians can and does exist independently of collective bargaining, just as it has among the general faculty. Historically, however, it is unlikely that the librarians' role in governance so frequently preceded collective bargaining, since organizing and acting as a faculty is a more recent experience for the librarians. It is perhaps too early to separate the experiments from the lasting systems. Cornell and Duke university librarians, for instance, have reorganized as faculties. The Central Michigan librarians began making personnel recommendations through various faculty committees before there was any mention of such procedures in its collective bargaining agreement. [27] At Oswego (SUNY), by-laws written by the librarians include provisions for the election and recall of the chairman of the library (which is a department at Oswego). Here again, the agreement did not create or mandate a faculty form of governance for the librarians. [28]

The librarians of the University of California (Berkeley), without full-fledged collective bargaining, developed a thorough-going plan which so clearly illustrates this whole set of aspirations that the main governance provisions are extracted here:[29]

2. Voice

Establish voice for librarians in library and University affairs through the following:

a. Regular participation by LAUC members in establishing University Library standards and forming policies governing their professional activities.

b. Representation by LAUC members on the Academic Senate Library Committees and the Library Council.

c. Participation by LAUC members on non-library-centered University committees.

3. Staff Meetings

a. Hold department and areas of service (e. g. , branch, public service departments and technical services departments) staff meetings on a regular basis, monthly or bi-monthly....

b. Schedule meetings of all librarians at least twice a year on each campus (and) review and discuss the next year's budget.

*　　　　*　　　　*

11. Rotating Heads of Departments

In departments where it is feasible, rotate heads of departments. Terms of office for these heads should be two or three years. The head should be chosen by the librarians in that department.

12. Evaluation of Administrative Personnel

Provide for all librarians to evaluate all administrative personnel regularly.

What is collective bargaining doing to advance aspirations of this sort? The Massachusetts system has shown some awkwardness in adapting to librarians. At Worcester State College, the college organization placed the library with the learning resources center, the latter headed by a non-librarian and comprising a professional staff that included both librarians and non-librarians. As the librarians alone could hardly exercise faculty governance over the entire center, they were somewhat frustrated in their desire to organize as a departmental faculty as other departments at Worcester were doing under the agreement. Southeastern Massachusetts University, in its agreement, simply excluded the library from the evaluation provisions for the faculty.

The agreement for 1974-77 between APSCUF and the Pennsylvania state colleges provides for a union-conducted election of a chairperson of each library. The agreement specifies only that this person be spokesman for the library faculty to the library director in all professional personnel matters. As two Westchester librarians have already written, interpretation of the chairperson's role is various. Is he/she a shop steward? Is the position analogous to a physics department chairman? The authors themselves appear to have had expectations far broader than the language of the agreement bears out, for they expect that this elected chairperson "would be responsible for implementing the collective bargaining contract."[30] This was the language of the union demand, but not of the agreement that was actually reached.

A recurring if sporadic aim in collective bargaining has been the election and recall of the library director by librarians in the bargaining unit. In a number of colleges and universities the department chairpersons are part of the bargaining unit, and of these a few are subject to some form of election and recall,[31] pursuant to a bargained agreement. Of course, as we have seen, a high degree of consultation, often tantamount to election, traditionally characterizes the selection of a department chairperson. Library directors or head librarians are treated in the administrative organization either as deans or as department chairpersons or heads, depending on the size and complexity of the institution in part. This treatment of the director has been a matter of administrative convenience rather than a conscious institutional recognition that the library is analogous functionally to either a school or department. One reason for desiring the election and recall of library directors was frankly stated by Belle Zeller, president of CUNY's faculty union: they would fight harder to get promotions for their faculty, and if they did not deliver they could be replaced.[32] A broader argument, where the director is a chairperson, is that librarians would be exercising a function enjoyed by the result of the faculty. The dispute at Worcester State College was complicated by the fact that the librarians were part of a "learning resources center" headed and partly staffed by non-librarians.

It is impossible at any given time to say that these are the only examples of direct influence by collective bargaining on library governance. Few governance provisions have been tailored to librarians: minor adaptations of promotion and tenure procedures, and in Pennsylvania the right to elect a "library chairperson" of uncertain role. For the most part, librarians have shared with faculty such gains as peer evaluation, grievance machinery and enforcement, and some protection from unbargained changes in status.

The times have interwoven three forms of participation: traditional faculty governance, traditional employee
powers under collective bargaining, and employee participation as a management technique. The sum of them is not
necessarily equal to the best parts of each. It remains to
be seen how far they are even compatible. Some advocates
of collective bargaining (e.g., AAUP) hope that imaginative
combinations of these forms can be devised that will at least
surpass any one of them alone. Others (e.g., AFT) view
collective bargaining as adequate and full of promise, sup-
planting other approaches.

Librarians in colleges and universities with ongoing
collective bargaining relationships have so far ridden along
with the faculty. That is not the case at Claremont, and it
need not be the invariable pattern of the future; but it is the
overwhelming experience up to 1976. The process has thus
brought librarians the traditional powers of collective bargaining, though as a minority within the unit. It has also
tended to reduce the distinctions between classroom faculty
and librarians, and shelters whatever gains in status the librarians have achieved with or without bargaining.

Collective bargaining has not spoken to the issues of
librarians' participation in the governance of either the library or the institution. Whatever solutions it may provide
must, as in all bargaining, be tolerable to both sides of the
table. As bargaining alters faculty governance, here adding
and there subtracting powers, librarians would be insensitive
to their changing environment if they did not examine and
re-examine the proposition that their needs will be largely
met by imitating the governance processes of the classroom
faculty. So far, resembling classroom faculty has proved
advantageous to the librarians who come under faculty

bargaining. It is important, however, that librarians be alert to changes in the role and goals of the faculty, and recognize that under certain circumstances a frank analysis of differences is as important as the quest for similarities.

Notes

1. David Kaser, "Modernizing the University Library Structure," College and Research Libraries, 31 (July, 1970) 227-231.

2. Maurice P. Marchant, "Participative Management as Related to Personnel Development," Library Trends, 20 (July, 1971) 49.

3. Beverly Lynch conveniently cites advocates and proponents of this view in her "Participative Management in Relation to Library Effectiveness," College and Research Libraries, 33 (Sept. , 1972) 384.

4. "Statement on Government of Colleges and Universities," AAUP Bulletin, 52 (Winter, 1966) 375-379.

5. Joseph Garbarino and Bill Aussieker, Faculty Bargaining: Change and Conflict. A Report Prepared for the Carnegie Commission on Higher Education and the Ford Foundation. McGraw-Hill, 1975, 278pp. 32-37. Also, Seymour M. Lipset, "Faculty Unions and Collegiality," Change, 7 (March, 1975) 39-41.

6. For example, Paul Strohm, "Faculty Input May Not Equal Output," Chronicle of Higher Education, 9 (Feb. 10, 1975) 24.

7. Belle Zeller, "Bargaining at the City University of New York," in Tice, op. cit. , 99-105.

8. Alfred D. Sumberg, "Should Faculties Organize?" in Tice, op. cit. , 117-127.

9. Donald Keck, "College Governance and Collective Bargaining," Today's Education 61 (Dec. , 1972) 51-52.

10. Dexter L. Hanley, "Issues and Models for Collective Bargaining in Higher Education," Liberal Education, 57 (March, 1971) 5-14.

11. New York Times, (Dec. 6, 1972) 42.

12. Joseph B. Garbarino, "Precarious Professors: New
     Patterns of Representation," Industrial Relations,
     10 (Feb., 1971) 1-20. Daniel R. Coleman, "The
     Evolution of Collective Bargaining as It Relates to
     Higher Education in America," CUPA Journal, 23
     (May, 1972) 8, 11.

13. James P. Begin, "Faculty Governance and Collective
     Bargaining: An Early Appraisal," ACBIS Special
     Report No. 5 (March, 1974) 11 pp. For a felici-
     tous overview of these tensions, see William B.
     Boyd, "The Impact of Collective Bargaining on Uni-
     versity Governance," AGB Reports, 16 (Nov.-Dec.,
     1973) 18-25. Also, Michael A. Falcone, "Collec-
     tive Bargaining: Its Effects on Campus Governance,"
     ACBIS Special Report No. 16 (Feb., 1975) 6 pp.
     Trevor Bain, "Academic Governance and Unions:
     The Case of CUNY," Industrial Relations, 14 (Feb.,
     1975) No. 1, 102-109, speaks to managerial re-
     sponsibility shifts caused by bargaining at CUNY.

14. Caesar Naples, "Collegiality and Collective Bargaining:
     They Belong Together," NCSCBHE Proceedings, 2nd
     Annual Conference, (April, 1974) 51-57. Lawrence
     De Lucia, "Collegiality and Collective Bargaining:
     Oil and Water," loc. cit. 58-60. Garbarino and
     Aussieker op. cit. 255. For the most recent work
     as of this writing, see Frank R. Kemerer and J.
     Victor Baldridge, Faculty Collective Bargaining and
     Academic Governance, soon to be published.

15. Chronicle of Higher Education, 8 (Nov. 26, 1973) 1.

16. Kenneth P. Mortimer, "A Survey of Experience in
     Academic Collective Bargaining." Typescript of
     address presented at ACRL, San Francisco, June,
     1975, 14-15.

17. Michigan Employment Relations Commission. Case
     No. C74-A19 (1974). For a general treatment of
     the problem, see B. J. Williams, "Faculty Bargain-
     ing: Exclusive Representation and the Faculty Sen-
     ate," CUPA Journal, 24 (Feb., 1973) 45-56.

18. Terrence N. Tice, "Pros and Cons of Academic

Collective Bargaining," in his Faculty Power: Collective Bargaining on Campus. Institute of Continuing Legal Education, Ann Arbor, 1972. 129-137. Also, Hanley, op. cit. , 9; and Henry L. Mason, "Faculty Unionism and University Governance," in Jack H. Schuster, ed. , Encountering the Unionized University. (New Directions for Higher Education) 2 (Spring, 1974) No. 1. 106 pp. 1-26.

19. Caesar J. Naples, "Collective Bargaining: Opportunities for 'Management'," in Schuster, op. cit. , 47-60. Also, Mason, op. cit. , 7.

20. Donald E. Walters, "Comment," College Management, (May, 1973) 6-7. Also in AGB Reports, 15 (March, 1973) 2-8.

21. Garbarino and Aussieker, op. cit. , 146; Bain, op. cit. , 106-107.

22. Neil S. Bucklew, "Collective Bargaining and Policy Making," Current Issues in Higher Education, 29 (1974) 136-141.

23. Begin, loc. cit. For a librarian's perspective, see Adeline Tallau and Benjamin R. Beede, "Faculty Status and Library Governance," Library Journal, 99 (June 1, 1974) 1521-1523. New Jersey Public Employment Relations Commission, Docket No. SN-12. Brief by Rutgers and Reply Brief by AAUP, 1975.

24. Kaser, loc. cit.

25. Ed Holley, "Who Runs Libraries? The Emergence of Library Governance in Higher Education," Wilson Library Bulletin 48 (Sept. , 1973) 42-50.

26. Richard De Gennaro recognized the assumption if only to doubt its validity. See his "Participative Management or Unionization?" College and Research Libraries, 33 (May, 1972) 173-174.

27. Cecily Johns Little, "Faculty Status and Collective Bargaining," Michigan Librarian, 41 (Fall, 1975) No. 7, 10-12.

28. "By-Laws of the Library Department," Penfield Library Faculty, SUNY at Oswego (June 11, 1974). Copy provided by courtesy of Alex F. Beattie.

29. University Council-American Federation of Teachers, "A Library Improvement Program for the University of California," Draft (Feb. 1, 1973). See also a similar proposal: University Federation of Librarians, "Library Improvement Program, University of California, Berkeley" (Aug. , 1968) 14 pp. , furnished through the kindness of Rudolf Lednicky.

30. Mary Anne Burns and Jeanette Carter, "Collective Bargaining and Faculty Status for Librarians: West Chester State College," College and Research Libraries, 36 (March, 1975) 115-120.

31. E. g. , Worcester, CUNY, St. John's.

32. N. Y. State Board of Education conference on librarians in collective bargaining, Syracuse, 1975.

Chapter 6

CONTRACT ADMINISTRATION

Contract administration means carrying out the bargained agreement. Nearly all of the provisions in such agreements place an obligation on management, and it is for management to administer the agreement. No matter what system of advice and internal government may exist at an institution, it is the employer who ultimately decides the personnel questions commonly covered by agreement. It is the employer who employs the new faculty member, determines and pays the salary, promotes the employee in rank or in classification; who reappoints or not; who assigns and changes duties; and who sets up calendars, schedules, and measures of work. From agreement to agreement, the discretion of the employer may be limited in any of these functions, but only the employer can carry them out.

Employee and Employer

The faculty in a bargaining relationship are treated as employees, and the employer's plea that faculty are not employees has been squelched by more than one labor decision.[1] Yet many faculty members have never considered themselves employees, but rather an integral and major part of the institution. If the term "employee" sits uncomfortably on some unionized faculty, the term "employer" has

its own ambiguities. The employer may be "the president
and fellows" of Harvard, "the regents" of Wayne State,
"the president and trustees" of Miami, or "the trustees"
of Central Michigan and hundreds of other colleges and universities, public or private. The employer may turn out
to be not the institution at all, but a state board: of regents, of education, or of higher education. The employer
can be an ecclesiastical body. A sharp distinction between
employer and employee is dissonant with academic traditions
that hold that, whatever legal formalities may occasionally
intrude, the faculty de facto manage the institution in at
least its main mission. These subtle gradations from employee to employer are threatened, not by superior argument or conscious choice on either side, but simply by the
proposition that no group can bargain collectively with itself.

Most of an agreement comprises employee rights of
some kind, though sometimes, too, unions have certain
rights distinct from those of the employees. (For example,
a union representative may have a seat on a college committee; or only the union may have authority to carry an
employee's grievance as far as arbitration; or union officials
may be given free time for union business.) Managements,
including universities, frequently assume that they retain all
rights not expressly conceded by agreement. [2] Nevertheless,
these are sometimes specified in "management rights"
clauses. The Oakland agreement, for example, states:

> Oakland has the legal responsibility and, subject
> to the terms of this Agreement, the right to man-
> age its operations, including but not limited to the
> right to (a) hire, assign, promote, demote,
> schedule, discipline, and discharge faculty mem-
> bers; (b) determine and schedule the academic
> year; (c) locate or relocate its physical facilities
> and equipment; (d) control all of its property.

Industrial unions are accustomed to management rights clauses, but an AAUP spokesman argues that, because the industrial model does not apply to colleges and universities, management rights clauses are inappropriate. [3]

Evaluation

The major academic personnel decisions rest on evaluation, coming primarily from peers. Peer evaluation is common practice in colleges and universities, and is implicit in the AAUP Statement. [4] It is variously described in about half the agreements. Rutgers, Central Michigan, New Jersey, SUNY, and Ferris, for example, do not explain their evaluation procedures in their agreements; CUNY, Worcester, Temple, Southeastern Massachusetts, and Oakland do. At Wayne State, which has other peer evaluation processes, the agreement describes only one for distributing merit awards.

Peer evaluation systems vary greatly. They need not be analyzed in detail for our present purposes, but the following questions show the permutations of possible systems, and may help those interested in setting up such a process:

Are the evaluations anonymous? Semi-anonymous (e.g., requiring a social security number)?

Do the evaluations require written statements of reasons?

Are they qualitative assessments, weighted ratings, or simply votes?

Are evaluations weighed according to the evaluator's knowledge?

Are evaluations within the same department

weighed the same as those from outside the department?

Do the questions go to professional and academic qualities, or are they of the bureaucratic sort?

Are evaluations by supervisors treated differently?

Are evaluations of supervisors treated differently?

What persons interpret peer evaluations?

How public are evaluations?

Evaluation procedures and criteria in agreements seldom, if ever, require reducing evaluation completely to a checklist or a counting of votes, although there are always those who would prefer rigidity. Unless the agreement plainly requires a mechanistic process and as plainly excludes other more meaningful assessments, there is no reason why the administrator should narrow the scope of evaluation. All evaluators in the system should exercise judgment and discretion to the maximum permitted under the agreement. If peers do not do so, there is no need for peer evaluation, and it will disappear.

Files

Personnel files are evidence in evaluation, as well as the repository of evaluations. They therefore arouse similar concerns, which may be summarized as questions of the following sort:

May the employee see his file?

What other persons are granted or denied access to it?

What does the employer put in the file?

May the employee put anything in it?

It is useful simply as a reference point to mention the practice of the Central Michigan University library, although the agreement itself has less to say about files:

The faculty member will be shown (not given) his personnel file at reasonable times.

Duly constituted colleague evaluation committees are encouraged to consult the files of persons under their consideration, but personal data occasionally made necessary by circumstances (e. g. , medical records supporting sick leave or disability claims) are not shown to these committees.

Strangers who do not claim authority (e. g. , credit investigators) are denied access to file information unless with the employee's express permission.

Strangers who claim authority (e. g. , police) are referred to the university attorney.

The employer places in the file whatever appears relevant to performance or to professional or intellectual abilities, except that materials submitted in confidence as references at the time of employment are not kept in the personnel file; nor are anonymous criticisms.

The faculty member may insert a reasonable amount of material in his file, such as commendations from others, or his own response to criticism.

Elsewhere, agreements occasionally spell out file practices. The SUNY agreement permits a person to examine his own file, and to have copies made from it, except for statements solicited in the process of considering reappointments or promotions. A union representative may also view the file, with the employee's permission. The employee is to be notified of any request from outside the university for file information, unless the notification is prohibited by law.

Under the New Jersey state colleges agreement, the employee is to receive a copy of every item inserted in his file. The employee or a union representative with his/her permission may view the file. The employee can insert commendations in the file. No anonymous material is to be placed in it.

CUNY recognizes two types of file, one containing original employment recommendations and references and not accessible to the employee, the other accessible to the employee and containing most other personnel records, including reports of observations of performance.

Temple's file clause is modeled on that of CUNY, with much the same wording. An important difference is that the observation reports are not accessible to the employee, but only to the committees and other persons responsible for reviewing the person's reappointment, promotion, or tenure.

Grievance and Arbitration

At the base of contract administration lies the grievance and appeals system by which each agreement is enforced. Minimally, grievance is the means by which the union or an employee can allege that the agreement has been violated, and, if investigation sustains the allegation, obtain a remedy.

Grievances sometimes afford the union a means of obtaining advantages that it could not achieve at the bargaining table. They have their political uses as well. Through grievances, the union may wish to emphasize issues intended

for the next round of negotiations, or reiterate and demonstrate its role as champion of its membership, or harry
both peers and administrators into abdicating their more
unpleasant duties. [5]

If grievances are a well-tempered weapon for the
clever, they are a deus ex machina to the naïve. It may indeed have been grievous for a college administration to convert a third of its crowded library space to deans' offices,
but the librarians ought to have known that it was not grievable under their union contract.

The grounds of grievance under agreements vary.
At Ferris, Wayne, and Central Michigan, for example, it
is essential to allege that some specific part of the agreement was violated by the employer. This basis is broadened
at SUNY, CUNY, the New Jersey colleges, Worcester,
Southeastern Massachusetts, and Rutgers, where alleged
violation of existing university or college policy is an added
opening to grievance machinery. Other grounds, such as
academic freedom, civil rights, and affirmative action, are
occasionally incorporated. The St. John's agreement incor-
porates the entire AAUP Statement by reference, thus making it all grievable. Temple and Oakland do not define
grievances.

Appeals systems for academic personnel decisions
were common before faculty collective bargaining. [6] Consequently, there is sometimes a standard grievance system
for alleged violations of the agreement, and a separate appeals route, inside or outside the agreement, for the faculty
member who is being terminated or disappointed in a promotion.

The stages of appeal may be numerous and time-
consuming, or simple and efficient. Over two-thirds have

three or four steps. More than half require the initial
raising of the issue within 20 days. They may go through
faculty committees or follow the administrative chain. [7]

Where the appeal ends is most important. [8] The
final decision in a grievance may lie with the governing
board of the institution, as at Rutgers and the New Jersey
and Massachusetts state colleges. Grievances unresolved
internally are referred to outside binding arbitration in many
cases, as at CUNY, Ferris, Monmouth, Oakland, Rhode Island College, St. John's, Southeastern Massachusetts, SUNY,
the University of Rhode Island, Wayne State, and the Pennsylvania state colleges. In some of these cases, however,
reappointment and promotion disputes are exempted from the
arbitration. The arbitrator's power may be limited variously from place to place. In the CUNY agreement, for
example, the arbitrator is not to substitute his judgment for
academic judgment. [9] That is, he may find that a physics
department violated its procedures; but he is not supposed
to decide that no matter what the physics faculty think, the
grievant is a good physics teacher. Another curb on arbitrators at CUNY limits the kind of remedy that they can fashion
for a grievant. Thus if the physics faculty denied a colleague tenure without following its procedures, the arbitrator
is supposed to remand the matter to the physics faculty to
reach a decision under proper procedures, or else to refer
the question to a university-wide faculty panel if a remand
seems unlikely to accomplish justice. What arbitrators are
not supposed to be able to do, which they did under an earlier CUNY agreement, is to order that the grievant be given
tenure.

Grievance procedures lend themselves to flow-chart-
ing, and because many librarians are familiar with this mode

of expression, it seems useful to illustrate important kinds
of grievance and appeal in this way (see pp. 95-100). As
they are illustrations, some may be slightly oversimplified,
as minor exceptions would obscure the major facts.

The bare bones of process, of course, do nothing to
reflect the substance of grievances. Few grievances are
ever made public, let alone published; but CUNY, which has
been so productive in this area, has published its earlier
arbitrations. [10]

The administrator of a faculty agreement has a
peculiar problem in that much of the decision-making in
personnel matters is entrusted to the faculty, who on the
whole exercise a preponderant influence in the substantive
judgments attending the employment, reappointment, tenure
and promotion of faculty members. [11] These substantive
judgments include both the establishment of criteria and
their application to individual cases. In exercising substantive judgments, however, faculty members also control the
most critical stages of procedure. The climate of the
times, especially under collective bargaining, places great
importance on procedure. Practically, most grievances are
founded on alleged procedural irregularities. The procedural
error may be material or not. It should surprise no one
that some grievants will clutch at straws and magnify harm-
less errors into the crucial issue at hand. As the critical
decisions are usually made by faculty, the execution or violation of procedures lies in their hands. That special
knowledge which justifies entrusting the faculty with substantive judgments does not always equip them to follow the
accompanying procedures. Procedures are bureaucratic,
faculty members often intensely anti-bureaucratic. A

(cont'd on p. 101)

Central Michigan University

Violation of Agreement

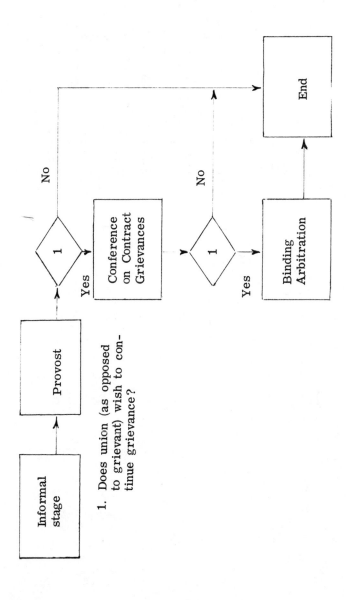

Informal stage

Provost

1. Does union (as opposed to grievant) wish to continue grievance?

No

Yes

Conference on Contract Grievances

No

Yes

Binding Arbitration

End

Central Michigan University

Appeals for Reappointment

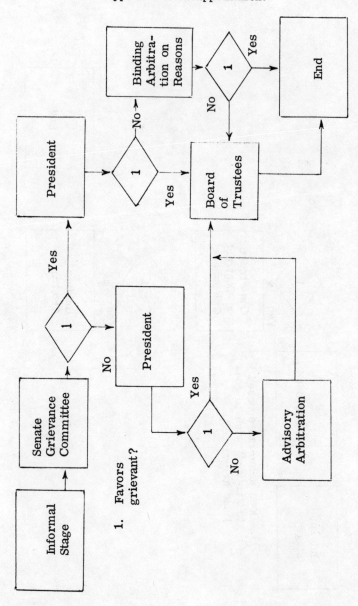

1. Favors grievant?

City University of New York

Violation of Agreement or Policies

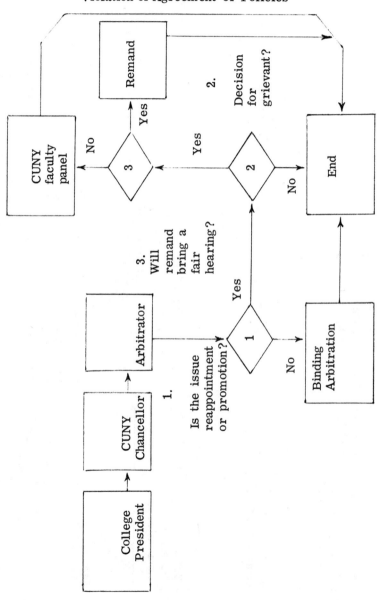

Temple

Various Grounds as Shown

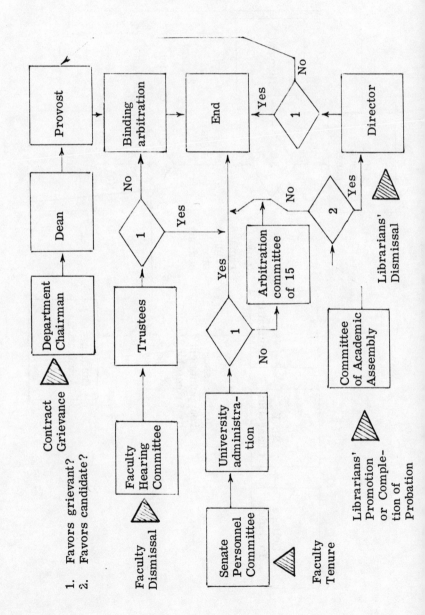

Rutgers

Violation of Agreement, or of Procedures
in Tenure and Promotion

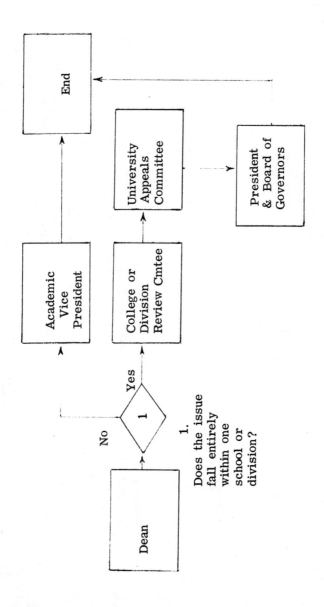

New Jersey State Colleges

Violation of Agreement or Policies

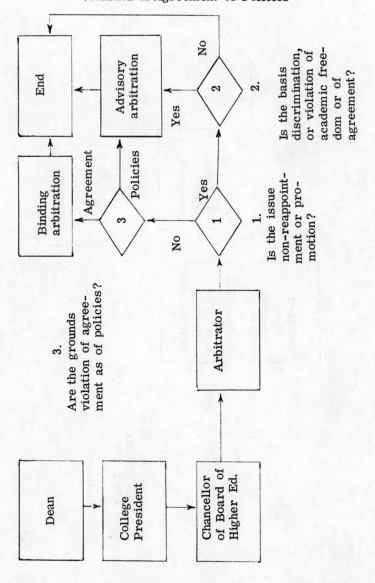

scholar may search his conscience to do justice to his colleagues and to uphold his profession, and yet disregard the letter of personnel procedures. The results of this system are that the administrator of the agreement is responsible for great areas of procedure over which he has no control, and that probably most faculty grievances against the administration are based on alleged lapses on the part of the grievant's colleagues. [12]

This conflict between procedural correctness and faculty style is not the only conflict in contract administration. Civil rights and affirmative action requirements can be violated by faculty committees. [13] These requirements can in turn conflict with the bargained agreement, so that the most sagacious of faculty committees cannot avoid appeals which they will sometimes lose.

Administrators

The new relationship may move, but also clarify, the line between employee and employer--the line at which their interests diverge. As the employer works through representatives who are themselves employees, there may be several tiers of employer-employee delineations, each bounding a set of interests. Each may be the first line of administration vis-à-vis a given bargaining unit. Presidents and deans are employees, but represent the employer to faculty bargaining units. Academic department heads or chairmen are sometimes in, sometimes out of, the faculty unit. [14] Within the library, the director may be a department chairman or a dean, depending on the organization of the institution and especially on whether it is a college or university. They are usually, however, first of all directors, and out of the bargaining unit.

Contract administration sorts administrators--not least of all library directors--through a new sieve. In the past, it has proved comfortable for many a university administration to allow the director to work in some isolation, and as a specialist. Sometimes it was assumed that the specialist-director had little general administrative competence, and so most library personnel and budget decisions were made above his head and outside of the library. At other times, it was assumed that the library was so esoteric an operation that the personnel decisions should be left to the director; then the president or provost had little way of knowing whether the director was a martinet, a passive nonentity, or a leader. Bargaining makes it dangerous for a university administration to be indifferent to the kind of library director it has. The martinet can generate expensive, avoidable grievances. The passive nonentity can allow practice to pile on practice, witlessly creating precedents deleterious to university policy. If the director is not a leader, possessing the peculiar skills of contract administration, no degree of technical expertise in librarianship can prevent the central university administration from assuming close control over personnel matters. If we suppose that ideally decisions on library personnel are best made within the library, then it is not desirable to have a void of this kind beckoning for more distant management.

If bargaining clarifies the role of most library directors, it clouds that of department heads within the library. In the familiar hierarchical organization of academic libraries, the latter have several roles:

> Leadership: They should incite and co-ordinate the initiative of those whom they lead.

Representation of viewpoints: They should effectively and truthfully express the views of their departments to the administration, and the views of the administration to their departments. This role requires credibility, logical and articulate communication, and the ability to appreciate other viewpoints.

Arbitration: They must occasionally impose a decision when consensus within the department is impossible, or when wider concerns transcend the wishes of the department.

Evaluation: With their special opportunities for observation, they bear a special responsibility in evaluating members of their departments.

Where the librarians have organized as a faculty, the relative emphases on these roles may change while the roles themselves continue. For example, peer evaluation ensures that the supervisor's opinion is not the only view we have of an employee, but the vantage points and special responsibility of the supervisor are still there to be reckoned with. Again, the two-way representation of viewpoints is more broadly shared in a faculty organization, without, however, eliminating the need for an able spokesman. Leadership continues to be a department head's role, even in a faculty organization. Department heads may or may not be able to function in arbitration; if they cannot, someone else does.

In academic departments such as history and physics, there is little if any supervision, for the members do not need to cooperate much; and of course a department chairman does not have superior knowledge in the sense that a head cataloger ought to have. William Axford's experience has suggested to him that department heads are a tier of negativism thwarting youthful enterprise, and his observation could well be true wherever they achieve their positions by seniority. [15]

They are sometimes supervisors, sometimes not.
Supervisors are excluded from the bargaining units comprising those whom they supervise, though they may form or
join another bargaining unit. All depends, however, on the
various tests of supervision. Under NLRB jurisdiction, a
supervisor is: "... any individual having authority, in the
interest of the employer, to hire, transfer, suspend, lay
off, recall, promote, discharge, assign, reward, or discipline other employees, or responsibly to direct them, or to
adjust their grievances, or effectively to recommend such
action, if in connection with the foregoing the exercise of
such authority is not of a merely routine or clerical nature,
but requires the use of independent judgment."[16] State labor
boards tend to have a more exacting definition of supervisor,
so that heads of library departments are usually included in
the unit with the other librarians.

Peer evaluation systems can place pressure on department heads. Some of it is salutary, but some systems
can impose on the head debilitating conflicts of interest. A
good department head must often make unpopular decisions
and change cherished routines. To make the supervisor's
reappointment contingent on a secret vote of those who had
been cherishing the routines does not encourage innovation
or decisive action. It does strengthen conservatives and
veto groups. They can remain silent in decision-making
sessions, when criticism would be timely and effective, in
order to enjoy the anonymity that the evaluation process
sometimes provides. This is the opposite of an academic
relationship. It is a part of contract administration to protect all persons, including department heads, from such
abuses as far as the agreement permits.

Contract administration need not be an obscure art. The administrator's task is to carry out his responsibilities to the institution while faithfully executing the terms of the agreement. These terms it is the administrator's problem to interpret. As academic administrators are seldom learned in the law, they must interpret as well-informed laymen. In difficult cases they usually have access to institutional legal counsel. The agreement, to say nothing of affirmative action and civil rights requirements, imposes new and sometimes undesirable formalities, which may excite among a few persons on both sides a morbid concentration on pseudo-legal niceties. The administrator can help all forgo these diversions; for though a faculty union agreement is normally born of an adversarial relationship, adversarial need not mean hostile. The relationship established by the agreement need not even be adversarial. Something of the old creativity and spontaneity is gone, but the administrator can preserve common sense, goodwill, and trustworthiness by displaying them himself.

Notes

1. As NLRB said of NYU in 1973, for instance (83 LRRM 1850) and of Fordham in 1971 (78 LRRM 1177).

2. Margaret K. Chandler and Connie Chiang, "Management Rights Issues in Collective Bargaining in Higher Education," NCSCBHE. Proceedings of the First Annual Conference, Baruch College, (April, 1973) 58-66. Also, Arthur A. Sloane and Fred Witney, Labor Relations. 2nd edition, Prentice-Hall, 1972. 554 pp. 395.

3. Alfred D. Sumberg, "Should Faculties Organize?" in Terrence N. Tice, ed., Faculty Power: Collective Bargaining on Campus. Institute of Continuing

Legal Education, Ann Arbor, 1972. 129-137.

4. "Statement on Government of Colleges and Univer-
    sities," AAUP Bulletin, 52 (Winter, 1966) 375-379.
    Also, "Model Statement of Criteria and Procedures
    for Appointment, Promotion in Academic Rank, and
    Tenure for College and University Librarians,"
    College and Research Library News, 34 (Sept. 1973)
    192-195.

5. James J. Healy, ed., Creative Collective Bargaining.
    Prentice-Hall, 1965. 294 pp. 14. Joseph W. Gar-
    barino and Bill Aussieker, Faculty Bargaining,
    Change and Conflict. Carnegie Foundation, 1975.
    278 pp. 256. Sloane and Witney (op. cit., 218)
    point out constructive cooperation in grievances.

6. Robert L. Williams, The Administration of Academic
    Affairs in Higher Education. U. of Michigan Press,
    1965. 182 pp. 16-22.

7. Tracy H. Ferguson and William L. Bergan, "Griev-
    ance-Arbitration Procedures and Contract Adminis-
    tration," Journal of College and University Law, 1
    (Summer, 1974) 374-375.

8. Maurice Benewitz and Thomas Mannix, "Grievance
    Procedures in Higher Education Contracts," Com-
    munity and Junior College Journal, 44 (Dec., 1973)
    22-24. Also, Bernard Mintz and Alan Golden,
    "Faculty Collective Bargaining and the Arbitral
    Process," CUPA Journal, 25 (July-Aug., 1974) 33-
    39.

9. Maurice C. Benewitz and Thomas M. Mannix, "The
    CUNY Grievance and Arbitration Experience: What
    Does It Teach about Collective Bargaining?"
    NCSCBHE. Proceedings of the Second Annual Con-
    ference. Baruch College (April, 1974) 61-69.

10. Board of Higher Education of the City of New York.
    Index, Digest, and Tables of Arbitration and Court
    Cases... Vol. 1: Cases Decided September 1, 1969
    through January 31, 1974. NCSCBHE, 1974. 216
    pp. Because the NCSCBHE is housed in Baruch
    College, and because CUNY has produced the major-
    ity of grievances, we know more about CUNY

grievances than any others. See: Charles Bob Simpson, "Academic Judgment and Due Process," NCSCBHE. Proceedings of the First Annual Conference, Baruch College, (April, 1973) 89-95. Thomas G. S. Christensen, "Due Process and Academic Judgment," NCSCBHE. op. cit. (1973) 104-108. Milton Friedman, "Special Issues in Arbitration of Higher Education Disputes: Academic Judgment and Tenure Quotas," NCSCBHE. Proceedings of the First Annual Conference, Baruch College, (April, 1973) 96-103. John C. Allen, comp., Bibliography on Grievance Procedure and Arbitration in Higher Education. National Center for the Study of Collective Bargaining in Higher Education. David Newton, "CUNY: A Grievous Story," paper presented at conference, "Academics at the Bargaining Table," Rutgers, 1972, 8 pp.

11. Trevor Bain, "Academic Governance and Unions: The Case of CUNY," Industrial Relations, 14 (Feb., 1975) 106. Also, Williams, op. cit., 2, 3, and 15.

12. Board of Higher Education of the City of New York, op. cit., and Garbarino and Aussieker, op. cit., 153.

13. Susan Fratkin, "Collective Bargaining and Affirmative Action," CUPA Journal, 26 (July-Aug., 1975) No. 3, 53-62.

14. Russell A. Smith, Harry T. Edwards, and R. Theodore Clarke, Jr., Labor Relations Law in the Public Sector. Bobbs-Merrill, 1974. 1222 pp. 272-273.

15. William Axford, "An Overlooked Cost of Achieving a Participatory Environment," College and Research Libraries, 35 (Jan., 1974) 5-6.

16. 29 U.S.C., sec. 152 (11) (1970).

Chapter 7

PROSPECTS

One purpose of this book has been to challenge the
assumptions of enthusiasts. It is also, however, meant as
an academic librarians' primer of collective bargaining:
not to make decisions for them but to help them make independent choices most suitable to their circumstances, on
those rare occasions when they have a choice. Naturally
the first thought of academic librarians is the direct impact
of bargaining on their role and personal welfare. That has
been almost the sole concern of the library literature on the
subject. Yet librarians are also affected when bargaining
touches libraries.

Libraries Bargained

Libraries themselves are bargained with faculty unions, often implicitly and sometimes explicitly. The most
common instance is the implicit competition for funds. If
increases in compensation exceed increases in available resources, the compensation part of educational expenditures
encroaches on the other parts, such as the library. This
shift is especially rapid because faculty compensation occu-
pies so large a proportion of the whole budget--often more
than 40%. If such a university or college is able to increase
its resources by only three per cent while the faculty union

succeeds in bargaining an eight per cent compensation increase, the proportion of faculty compensation will have
risen from 40% to 43. 2% in a single year. The reciprocal
amount from which come all other expenses will have dropped
from 60% to 56. 8% in proportion; and the absolute amount
available for these purposes will have dropped by 1. 5%.
At the same time, inflation has not visited employees alone,
but practically the employer's entire budget, including microscopes, heat, and books. A union may propose increases
in the library book budget. In most cases, however, the
total cost of a bargained agreement comes from a single
pool, so that all items are competitive and the union must,
at least in petto, assign priorities to them. Only at Oakland
did the unusual presence of interest arbitration hold out to
the union the prospect of exacting an improved book budget
that did not directly compete with compensation demands.

The Oakland AAUP proposed a restoration of a severe
cut in the library book budget, and adhered to its stand
throughout negotiations. The university administration declined to negotiate the issue. As so often in academe, the
line between educational policy and working conditions was
unclear. The union contended that the size of the acquisitions budget was a condition of employment for the faculty,
inasmuch as teaching performance as well as opportunities
for research and therefore promotion depended on an adequate
library. The university contended that this, like all alloca-
tions of resources, was a managerial prerogative. The arbitrator, though commenting that the union had presented
substantial evidence to show that this decision of the university administration was unwise, held that the cut had not
eroded the library so far as to make it an untenable working
condition.

Are book budgets, then, a mandatory subject of bargaining? That would seem to depend on the severity of their inadequacy, and on the degree to which an arbitrator is persuaded of the importance of the library as a working condition. Would book budgets improve if they were a mandatory subject of bargaining? There is no reason to suppose so. Whatever can be bargained upward can be bargained downward, and whatever becomes a counter on the bargaining table can be traded for other counters such as salary.

Other library conditions could be subject to bargaining, perhaps mandatory, perhaps not: the loan period for faculty members, for instance, or perhaps faculty study space. If such issues as library hours or the selection of library books drew sufficient interest on a campus, they might well work their way onto the bargaining table, but they are small compared with the main concerns of bargaining.

Trades unions tend to save for their own members the kind of work they perform. Thus carpenters erect wooden shelving, but only steel workers steel shelving. So far, the only example of such a clause affecting academic librarians appears in the Oakland agreement:

ARTICLE III

WORK OF THE BARGAINING UNIT

3. All professional library service and the teaching of credit courses shall be the exclusive work of the bargaining unit, provided that any person granted faculty rank, and visiting lecturers may teach credit courses on a part-time basis.

Libraries increasingly farm out certain kinds of professional library service. Approval plans are a way of subcontracting certain acquisitions functions. To computer

networks such as OCLC libraries sub-contract certain cata-
loging functions. To others, libraries sub-contract literature searches. In each case there is a potential impact on
the bargaining unit members. The impact may be benign,
liberating them from routine; or it may jeopardize their employment or expectations for advancement. One such person
adversely affected may grieve, if there is a restrictive
clause, and thus start a process which nowhere consults a
consensus of professional opinion, but simply examines
whether the union agreement has been violated or not. The
use of paraprofessionals is another area in which the dis-
agreement by one librarian under such a clause over what
is and is not professional could engender a grievance the
outcome of which would be independent of the desires of the
librarians and of the needs of the library.

Libraries have been bargained in other respects as
well, as for example at Worcester State and some other
Massachusetts state colleges where the college library committee, among others, is composed of one-third faculty,
one-third administration, and one-third student members.

Goals and Minorities

The achievements of bargaining, whether collective
or individual, are the product of one's power and goals.
Power in collective bargaining must be understood broadly
as something that can include sweet reason and public sym-
pathy as well as the ability to maintain or withstand strikes,
and as something that is modified by the power and goals of
the adversary. Increased power to achieve certain goals
is, of course, the whole purpose of collective bargaining,
but the very process alters the goals. Collective bargaining

revises goals as increased power raises aspirations, and as union expertise leads members to focus on specific measures such as cost-of-living clauses. It revises goals by reinvesting some power for the purpose of further increasing power, as for instance when a union bargains an agency shop clause. It revises goals, too, by reducing them to the common rule, so that individual desires are bent in an effort to achieve the greatest good for the greatest number of bargaining unit members.

Although the common rule is a source of union strength, the special goals of minorities have to be pretty inexpensive to prevail in this system. Academic librarians are a perennial minority, between four and ten per cent of the unit, and must expect considerable frustration as a result.

Goals and priorities are established via the union's own political system, which may or may not be sensitive to minorities, and may or may not be democratic. Thus members bargain first with their own union, whether weakly or strongly, and recapitulate internally the formula which states that achievements are the product of goals and power. This process is, of course, further complicated in a system-wide union. State and national affiliations, moreover, can pursue goals that conflict with those of the union. For example, the NEA, dominated as it is by K-12 teachers, actively lobbies to restrict the production of new teachers in ways inimical to the interests of faculty in colleges and universities that produce school teachers. These faculty members are not infrequently represented by an agent affiliated with NEA, and where certain forms of agency shop prevail, these same faculty members find themselves compelled to contribute substantial sums to lobby against their own interests and beliefs.

After passing through the union, the surviving goals are bargained with the administration. Now the sense of frustration is heightened among the general membership by the usual secrecy of the bargaining table and caucus. A sophisticated union team, by role-playing, can give its own interest groups an understanding of the trials that their wishes must pass in negotiations. Others allow themselves to be cast in the role of the department store Santa, listening affably but not delivering the goods.

Librarians are not only a minority, but usually part of Coleman's "subpopulation," on whom collective bargaining in its leveling way is bestowing privileges previously reserved to faculty. Librarians are among the less privileged groups in their faculty units. They therefore stand to gain from general egalitarian achievements in bargaining. These are: grievance machinery, increased job security for the untenured, and the entrenchment of practices previously enjoyed. As long as librarians are a minority, there is always a danger that they can suffer from oversight, as for example where librarians in a faculty unit do not enjoy tenure and the agreement requires retrenchment among the nontenured before it can occur among the tenured. On the other hand, their monetary gains under collective bargaining have occurred more by oversight than persuasion.

Shifting goals of the faculty require a continuing reexamination of goals by the librarians. One commonly perceived goal of librarians in faculty units has been the sharing or displacement of administrative authority, and this in turn the librarians usually view as their assuming faculty privileges in governance, with a consequent modification or replacement of a hierarchical structure by a faculty structure. Because shared authority is so familiar a model in academe, union goals superficially appear to replicate it; yet authority shared with a union serves purposes quite different from those of faculty-administration sharing outside of collective bargaining. Thus some long-sought aspects of faculty status are likely to elude librarians who pursue them by this means. There is, as we have seen, dispute as to whether collective bargaining can achieve this end at all. One side argues that collective bargaining alone has the power to force a transfer of administrative functions to the bargaining unit, reducing administrators to a kind of secretariat with little voice in policy. Another side argues that the nature and history of collective bargaining do not bear out this speculation, and that if anything a sharper distinction forms between employee and employer, shifting even previously shared authority into the canon of management rights. Charles Ping once epitomized the argument thus: "The sense of the discussion seemed to be that collective bargaining and university governance are compatible if labor negotiations become something other than labor negotiations and if university governance is dramatically altered."[1]

Academic Librarians Alone

Although we have much experience with librarians in faculty units, future determinations of bargaining units may place academic librarians in a different situation. At the University of Chicago, they may find themselves in a unit of non-supervisory librarians partly resembling the Claremont unit. There is no predicting at this writing what bargaining unit or units will emerge at Berkeley. Still less clear is the development of librarians' bargaining units at other major research universities. Faculty bargaining has tended to concentrate in colleges and universities of the AAUP classes IIA and IIB; that is, those with largely master's level or bachelor's level programs. At class I (major research) universities, attempts to adopt an agent for the faculty have not been frequent, and where made have succeeded only half the time. This, plus the fact that prestigious faculties may press for a "pure" unit even if they do adopt bargaining, suggests that any needs that the librarians feel for collective bargaining will have to be met in one of the following ways:

> 1) A unit of the Claremont type, combining non-professional library employees with non-supervisory professional librarians;

> 2) A unit of non-faculty academic professionals, as if the SUNY unit were purged of classroom faculty; or

> 3) A unit composed only of professional librarians (including or excluding supervisors, according to jurisdiction).

Whatever benefits may come from such units, each would, it seems, put an end locally to any prospect of acquiring familiar faculty roles and privileges. Whether to abandon these aspirations depends on pragmatic considerations such as what other benefits can be expected from collective bargaining, and the prognosis of the local librarians ever achieving full faculty status in any event.

The examples of public libraries of Claremont and of unionized Canadian academic librarians (also a useful perspective) strongly suggest that academic librarians would not win recognition or benefits commensurate with those of faculty in any bargaining unit that does not include the faculty.

Profession and Bargaining Unit

The determination of the bargaining unit can further affect academic librarians by dividing them into members and non-members. The example of Claremont shows how far this division can go, splitting the professional librarians roughly in half. Even in state jurisdictions library directors, and usually assistant directors, are excluded from the unit. As a result both members and non-members become confused about their roles. Are governance committees limited to bargaining unit members or are they meant to include all professional librarians? Which is desirable? Are personnel committees so limited, and if so, are they precluded from any but formal communication with the director and other non-members? To what extent can or should free discussion be held between unit members and non-members on issues directly affecting terms and conditions of employment? Or affecting other professional concerns?

These role problems have an impact on the profession. If unit determination truly divides some librarians from others in these areas, then the profession is redefined so as to depend on membership in a bargaining unit. When the arts of administration and management cease to form a part of librarianship, they will be practiced by non-librarians. As a group of California academic librarians have written, "The realization of librarianship as a specialized management profession is not, we admit, a universally shared objective. We urge, however, that it be universally considered." If a professional association were to join an external group against the administration, "In one fell swoop we will have achieved, as professionals, permanent self-identification as an employee group-contra-management and regained our forty-hour [week] with business (you can be sure) as usual."[2]

It is therefore an oversimplification to describe collective bargaining as a contest in which the union champions the professionalism of librarians against an administration bent on regimenting them. Academic librarians have struggled with the faculty as well as with administrations for recognition of the level of their services. The attitude of AFT is that collective bargaining suffices unto itself, and it is irrelevant whether it encourages professionalism. Others advise academic librarians to shift their attention from status to the securities and economic benefits that are the usual goals of collective bargaining.[3]

Arguments that collective bargaining on campus advances professionalism run as follows:

> 1. Without a high sense of security, professionals cannot devote the full measure of their attention to their calling and the pursuit of knowledge. Worry is fatal to the creativity and dedication essential to high professionalism.

> 2. Affluence characterizes professionals.

> 3. Academic freedom, another essential part of professionalism, must be safeguarded by sanctions more powerful than those available before collective bargaining appeared on campus.

> 4. Security and academic freedom aside, it is still repugnant to the professional to operate in an environment polluted by the arbitrary and capricious exercise of authority. By enforcing due process, collective bargaining again advances professionalism.

> 5. Implicit in professional status is the ability to set goals, judge means, and evaluate colleagues and programs. Collective bargaining defends and advances these powers.

6. A profession cannot long survive a persistent decline in the quality of those who elect to enter it. The knowledge that these guarantees are underwritten by collective bargaining will attract those of high quality.

7. The institution, knowing that it is less free to correct original errors in hiring, will advance the level of professionalism by taking greater care in hiring.

8. It is characteristic of both a bargaining unit and a profession to exclude non-members from performing the functions of members.

Arguments that collective bargaining discourages professionalism run along the following lines:

1. Collective bargaining tends to eliminate all material rewards for excellence in the profession, thus discouraging able and enterprising persons from entering or even remaining in it.

2. The blind protection of the least competent in the name of job security can never promote professionalism.

3. The judgment of colleagues is critical in many professional decisions, but bargained grievance procedures interfere with the exercise of such judgments, by intimidating peers, requiring their attention to minuscule technicalities, translating the language of academic discussion into legalisms, and subjecting professional judgments to review by labor arbitrators.

4. Union goals teach implicitly that excellence, dedication, and innovation beyond the common rule are mere gifts to the employer.

5. It is the union's responsibility to optimize the wages, hours, and working conditions of its constituency, regardless of whether these are consistent with professional goals.

6. The kind of person who prefers collective to

individual bargaining is unlikely to represent the most promising material in any profession.

7. Academics should close off no part of their work from free discussion (compare the debate over classified research); but collective bargaining attempts to limit some subjects to a single, often restricted, forum.

8. The level of polemics in collective bargaining is itself incompatible with unprejudiced inquiry.

9. The securities of collective bargaining tend to make duties more specific and more difficult to adapt to changing needs, and thus detract from the flexibility of the professional to devise new responses to new situations.

These arguments on both sides go to the substance rather than the trappings of professional status. Many of them can be traced to a tension inherent in professionalism, the accommodation of personal interests with the interests of the client or employer. A non-professional is not required to exercise extensive judgment in weighing these interests. To arrive by eight, to depart at five, and only between those hours to perform defined functions at prescribed levels of competence: these are typical of what the non-professional, however skillful, owes the employer. The employee has few conflicts of interest in serving the employer, and consequently feels little burden to resolve them. Such conflicts, however, consistently characterize the professional. Although some are removed from the professional's judgment (salary, for example), most are left in the first instance squarely to him or her to resolve, with or without the oversight of ethics committees. Every specification designed to resolve this tension, whether it is a detailed job description or a clause in a bargained agreement, removes some of this privilege-burden and dilutes this important ingredient of professionalism.

It is harder for librarians to discuss their professionalism when they treat it as an absolute which is totally possessed by the blessed and lacking among the damned. It is rather a spectrum. Along this spectrum some professionals are more and some are less typically so than librarians, and some librarians are more professional than other librarians. These characteristics depend in part on the attitudes and abilities of the individual, and in part on the nature of the work. Collective bargaining, because it influences these elements, can move librarians to or fro along the spectrum, or off it entirely.

Professional Associations

The probable inability of ALA or ACRL to function as a bargaining agent for academic librarians does not end the story of their interaction with collective bargaining. Their possible roles I described in an earlier article:

"1) The professional association might oppose all collective bargaining among college and university librarians. In the clamor among adversaries, the union is unwilling, and the administration usually forbidden, to present arguments on this side of the question. A professional association could fill this vacuum, and become the librarians' only mentor against unionism. The underlying theory, that professionalism and unionism are incompatible, is not so much invalid as moot, in view of the respectable boudoirs such as Rutgers where the cohabitation is accepted.

"2) The professional association might take a neutral position. Neutrality could all too easily result from timidity or inertia, but it could also come from a careful weighing of the interests of the profession. A courageous neutrality could provide parallel support for librarians in any given cause, whether the support casts the association with a union or with an administration. This course has its precedents in earlier AAUP policy, and closely matches the principles-and-sanctions system. It is doubtful how far the leisurely support of most such associations can help either bargainer in its intensely tactical approach to problems. Yet, just as AAUP principles appear widely in bargaining even where AAUP is not the agent, this kind of influence may still be possible.

"3) Associations might help librarians get into faculty units. Although inclusion does not assure librarians of equality with other faculty members, exclusion perpetuates their inequality. Local situations must ultimately indicate whether inclusion is desirable. If it is, there comes a time on campus when the association can seek to persuade the administration or union to accept librarians into the bargaining unit. If one of the parties still demurs, there comes another time for such persuasion before some labor board hearing. Of six disputes that came before NLRB, the administration opposed the inclusion of librarians in four cases; the union opposed their inclusion in one; and in a sixth, one rival union opposed inclusion of librarians and the other was indifferent. At Youngstown, Saginaw, Delaware, and Ashland, librarians were excluded from the faculty unit not by any labor board but ultimately by inaction or consent of the parties. An early exclusion of librarians from the Rutgers AAUP unit was remedied through the close relationship of the librarians with their colleagues in the academic senate. Although librarians usually get into faculty units now, there is obviously room for more effort.

"4) An association might exert influence on behalf of librarians in any union where they are a minority. It is hard to imagine a union being swayed by fear of ACRL sanctions against the employer, but the short history of faculty bargaining does furnish examples of the influence of professional groups on the union. The biologists within the Pennsylvania state colleges union (APSCUF) organized and gained a workload concession. Unions have often incorporated in their demands the principles and even the language of AAUP. The Library Association of the City University of New York (LACUNY) has been something of a union within the union, vigorously if not always successfully asserting the case for librarians.

"5) Associations might provide leadership and guidance for academic librarians' unions. ACRL's nine "Rights and Privileges" might be useful to such unions as just one more voice for a good cause. Bargained agreements, however, show a great deal of local color, centering on campus-wide or at most system-wide concerns. The unions are ahead of ACRL in those matters of most interest to them, and are more likely to provide timely leadership than to need it.

"6) A librarians' association might foster itself as the bargaining agent, as some AAUP chapters have recently done. Here, however, the differences between AAUP and ACRL become critical. For example, it seems impossible for a librarians' association ever to represent any but librarians, or at most library employees. So far it seems unlikely that librarians would fare better in their own union than in a faculty union, although some in the Pennsylvania and Massachusetts state college systems feel otherwise. We have yet to see what an aggressive group like the California

Library Association might attempt or achieve if public employee bargaining becomes legal there. A system-wide or
state-wide bargaining unit of academic librarians remains
an untested possibility. "[4]

Although collective bargaining may sharpen criticism
of domination of these associations by administrators, the
ACRL is voicing some of the goals of bargaining agents,
and there is no reason to suppose that the views of administrators will receive much heed in the associations as these
expressions continue.

Perhaps the broad view of Haug and Sussman makes
the questions unimportant: "The fact is that professionals
like engineers, teachers, nurses, social workers, and others
who work in organizations, are turning to unionism, with or
without the consent of their appropriate professional association and with apparent disregard for differences in goal emphases or values.... "[5]

At one end of the scale of colleges and universities
the structures of academic governance are so frail, the
spirit of free inquiry so mean, the administration so alien,
and the dignity of the professoriate so atrophied, that collective bargaining can scarcely fail to bring improvement.
At the other end of the scale, where these traits are re-
versed, collective bargaining may offer no advantage at all.
Academic librarians can assess their lot by this scale or by
a scale of their own devising. If in doing so they weigh their
welfare and their professional role, they will have achieved
more self-analysis than in their years of brooding over
status.

Notes

1. Charles J. Ping, "On Learning to Live with Collective Bargaining," Journal of Higher Education, 44 (February, 1973) 103-113.

2. Dora Biblarz, et al., "Professional Associations and Unions: Future Impact of Today's Decisions," College and Research Libraries, 36 (March, 1975) 121-128.

3. William D. Hayward, NJEA official, quoted in Library Journal, 96 (May 15, 1971) 1662-1664. See also Virginia Lee Lussier, "National Faculty Associations in Collective Bargaining," ACBIS Special Report No. 8. 15 pp.

4. John W. Weatherford, "Professional Associations and Bargaining Agents," Library Journal, 100 (January 15, 1975) 99-102.

5. Marie R. Haug and Marvin B. Sussman, "Professionalization and Unionism, a Jurisdictional Dispute?" American Behavioral Scientist, 15 (March-April, 1971) 528.

Chapter 8

SELECT BIBLIOGRAPHY

For any subject in such flux as academic collective bargaining, a bibliography should begin with ongoing information services such as the following:

The Academic Collective Bargaining Information Service in Washington is sponsored by the Association of American Colleges. Its chief function is to develop and publish information for those familiar with academic governance and administration but not with faculty bargaining. Some of these materials are also made available through ERIC and the Association of Research Libraries. A number of ACBIS pamphlets have been cited in this book. The first of an ACBIS Monograph Series appeared in 1975.

The National Center for the Study of Collective Bargaining in Higher Education, housed at Baruch College, concentrates on research in the area. The Center boasts a highly current collection of agreements, and produces KWIC indexes to them. NCSCBHE publishes a bi-monthly newsletter, an updated list of union agreements with four-year and two-year colleges and universities, and bibliographies (described elsewhere). The Center also publishes the Proceedings of its annual conferences, to which this book makes numerous citations.

Since 1968, the National Education Association has

published its Negotiation Research Digest, a monthly survey
of rulings, negotiations, legislation, and other information
affecting NEA's constituency. For our area it partly over-
laps Government Employees Relations Report, a weekly since
1963, published by the Bureau of National Affairs.

The University Student Senate of CUNY in 1975
funded a Research Project on Students and Collective Bargaining, which is housed in Washington. Its Monthly Reports keep pace with bargaining developments in higher education, and especially those concerning students.

The Industrial Relations Center of the University of
Hawaii publishes a Higher Education Contract Clause Finder
(2nd issue, January 1974, unpaged).

BIBLIOGRAPHIES

John C. Allen, Collective Bargaining in Higher Education,
1971-73. Bibliography No. 1 (April, 1973). National
Center for the Study of Collective Bargaining in Higher
Education. 57 pp.

John C. Allen, V. Ariyabuddiphongs, and I. A. Weitzman,
Collective Bargaining in Higher Education. Bibliography
No. 2 (April, 1974). National Center for the Study of
Collective Bargaining in Higher Education. 109 pp.

John C. Allen and Daniel J. Julius, Higher Education Col-
lective Bargaining: Other Than Faculty Personnel. 1
(Dec., 1974). National Center for the Study of Collective
Bargaining in Higher Education. 53 pp.

Margaret A. Chaplan, "Collective Bargaining in Libraries:
A Bibliography," in Frederick A. Schlipf, ed., Collective
Bargaining in Libraries. Allerton Park Institute No. 20.
University of Illinois, 1975. 146-164.

Alan C. Coe, "Collective Bargaining with Faculty," CUPA
Journal, 24 (Sept., 1973) No. 4, 1-25. Bibliography,
18-25.

John W. Gillis, "The Continuing Development of Academic Collective Bargaining," Liberal Education, 57 (Dec., 1971) 529-539.

Nancy Huling, "Faculty Status--A Comprehensive Bibliography," College and Research Libraries, 34 (Nov., 1973) 440-462.

Daniel J. Julius and John C. Allen, Collective Bargaining in Higher Education. Bibliography No. 3 (April, 1975). National Center for the Study of Collective Bargaining in Higher Education. 130 pp.

Joan D. North, Collective Bargaining in Higher Education. Bibliography No. 2 (Aug., 1972). Manpower and Industrial Relations Institute, University of Alabama. 10 pp.

Terrence N. Tice, Resources on Academic Bargaining and Governance. Academic Collective Bargaining Information Service, Washington D.C. Published by ERIC Clearing House on Higher Education, July, 1974. 42 pp.

BOOKS AND ARTICLES

Books and articles on faculty collective bargaining and related developments (including those among academic librarians) are affected by the currency of the topic. It is thus easy to confine the central bibliography to publications of the past six years; but the pioneer, whose contribution is timely only at great cost of energy, is condemned to early obsolescence.

The list of authors includes both practitioners and detached observers. Because the subject is academic collective bargaining, rather than teamsters' or garment workers', a higher proportion of the practitioners bear impressive academic credentials. For the same reason, they articulate and publish their observations beyond the desires of non-academic practitioners to do so. On the other hand, they suffer from the fact that those who make history sometimes lack the time to write it.

This section on books and articles is divided into a main part, Academic Collective Bargaining, and three background parts: Colleges and Universities, Librarians, and Employee Relations. The main part is arranged chronologically, the rest alphabetically.

Academic Collective Bargaining

1971

James P. Begin and Jack Chernick, "Collective Bargaining Agreements in Colleges and Universities: Grievance and Job Allocation Provisions," CUPA Journal, 22 (May, 1971) 52-63.

Matthew W. Finkin, "Collective Bargaining and University Government," AAUP Bulletin, 57 (Summer, 1971) 149-162.

Joseph B. Garbarino, "Precarious Professors: New Patterns of Representation," Industrial Relations, 10 (February, 1971) 1-20.

Dexter L. Hanley, "Issues and Models for Collective Bargaining in Higher Education," Liberal Education, 57 (March, 1971) 5-14.

John C. Hepler, "Timetable for Takeover," Journal of Higher Education, 42 (February, 1971) 103-115.

William F. McHugh, "Collective Bargaining with Professionals in Higher Education: Problems in Unit Determination," Wisconsin Law Review, 55 (1971) no. 1, 55-90.

Gus Tyler, "The Faculty Join the Proletariat," Change, 3 (Winter, 1971-72) 44.

William Van Alstyne, "Tenure and Collective Bargaining," Current Issues in Higher Education, 26 (1971) 210-217.

1972

Daniel R. Coleman, "The Evolution of Collective Bargaining

as It Relates to Higher Education in America," CUPA Journal, 23 (March, 1972) 40-60; and 23 (May, 1972) 1-19.

Council of Chief Librarians (CUNY), "Recommendations Regarding New Contract for Instructional Staffs," LACUNY Journal, 1 (Winter, 1972) 35.

Joseph Garbarino and Bill Aussieker, "Faculty Unionism: From Theory to Practice," Industrial Relations, 11 (February, 1972) 1-21.

Donald Keck, "College Governance and Collective Bargaining," Today's Education, 61 (December, 1972) 51-52.

J. David Kerr and Kenneth Smythe, "Bargaining Issues," in Terrence N. Tice, ed., Faculty Power: Collective Bargaining on Campus, Institute of Continuing Legal Edution, Ann Arbor, 1972, 315-317.

J. David Kerr and Kenneth M. Smythe, "Collective Bargaining in Public Institutions," in Terrence N. Tice, ed., Faculty Power: Collective Bargaining on Campus. Institute for Continuing Legal Education, Ann Arbor, 1972, 54-56.

David Newton, "CUNY, a Grievous Story." Paper presented at conference, "Academics at the Bargaining Table," Rutgers, 1972. 8 pp. Also in ERIC, ED 082 701, October, 1973.

"Position Paper Submitted to and Approved by the Negotiating Committee of the Legislative Conference of the College of the City of New York on March 2, 1972," LACUNY Journal, 1 (Spring, 1972) 29-30.

Alfred D. Sumberg, "Should Faculties Organize?" in Terrence N. Tice, ed., Faculty Power: Collective Bargaining on Campus. Institute of Continuing Legal Education, Ann Arbor, 1972, 129-137.

Terrence N. Tice, ed., Faculty Power: Collective Bargaining on Campus. Institute of Continuing Legal Education, Ann Arbor, 1972, 368 pp.

Belle Zeller, "Bargaining at the City University of New York," in Terrence N. Tice, ed., Faculty Power:

Collective Bargaining on Campus. Institute of Continuing Legal Education, Ann Arbor, 1972, 99-105.

1973

Bill Aussieker and Joseph W. Garbarino, "Measuring Faculty Unionism: Quantity and Quality," Industrial Relations, 12 (May, 1973) 117-124.

James P. Begin, Academics at the Bargaining Table: Early Experience. ERIC, ED 082 701, October, 1973.

William B. Boyd, "The Impact of Collective Bargaining on University Governance," AGB Reports, 16 (November-December, 1973) 18-25.

Michael Brick, ed., Collective Negotiations in Higher Education. ERIC, ED 084 993, 1973.

Robert K. Carr and Daniel K. Van Eyck, Collective Bargaining Comes to Campus. Washington, A. C. E., 1973.

E. Daniel Duryea and Robert S. Fisk, Faculty Unions and Collective Bargaining. Jossey-Bass, 1973.

Clarence R. Hughes, et al., ed., Collective Negotiations in Higher Education: A Reader. Blackburn College Press, 1973.

Everett Carll Ladd, Jr., and Seymour M. Lipset, Professors, Unions, and Higher Education. Carnegie Commission, 1973.

Everett Carll Ladd, Jr., and Seymour M. Lipset, "Unionizing the Professoriate," Change, 5 (Summer, 1973) 42.

Charles J. Ping, "On Learning to Live with Collective Bargaining," Journal of Higher Education, 44 (February, 1973).

Terrence N. Tice and Grace W. Holmes, ed., Faculty Bargaining in the Seventies. Ann Arbor, Institute of Continuing Legal Education, 1973.

Donald E. Walters, "Comment," College Management, (May, 1973) 6-7; also in AGB Reports, 15 (March, 1973) 2-8.

B. J. Williams, "Faculty Bargaining: Exclusive Representation and the Faculty Senate," CUPA Journal, 24 (February, 1973) 45-56.

1974

G. Alan Balfour, "More Evidence That Unions Do Not Achieve Higher Salaries for Teachers," Journal of Collective Negotiations in the Public Sector, 3 (1974) no. 4, 289-304.

James P. Begin, "Faculty Governance and Collective Bargaining: An Early Appraisal," ACBIS Special Report no. 5, (March, 1974) 11 pp.

Robert Birnbaum, "Unionization and Faculty Compensation," Educational Record, 55 (Winter, 1974) 29-33.

William W. Boyer, "The Role of Department Chairmen in Collective Bargaining: The University of Delaware Experience," CUPA Journal, 25 (April, 1974) 49-54.

Neil S. Bucklew, "Collective Bargaining and Policy Making," Current Issues in Higher Education, 29 (1974) 136-141.

Lawrence De Lucia, "Collegiality and Collective Bargaining: Oil and Water," NCSCBHE Proceedings, 2nd Annual Conference (April, 1974) 58-60.

Education Commission of the States. Collective Bargaining in Postsecondary Educational Institutions. Applications and Alternatives in the Formulation of Enabling Legislation. Report no. 45 (March, 1974) 104 pp.

Tracy H. Ferguson and William L. Bergan, "Grievance-Arbitration Procedures and Contract Administration," Journal of College and University Law, 1 (Summer, 1974) 374-375.

Ellis Katz, "Faculty Stakes in Collective Bargaining: Expectations and Realities," in Jack H. Schuster, ed., Encountering the Unionized University. New Directions for Higher Education, no. 5 (Spring, 1974) 30.

C. Gregory Lozier, "Changing Attitudes Towards the Use of Strikes in Higher Education," CUPA Journal, 25 (April, 1974) 41-48.

C. Gregory Lozier and Kenneth P. Mortimer, Anatomy of a Collective Bargaining Election in Pennsylvania's State-Owned Colleges. Center for the Study of Higher Education, Pennsylvania State University, 1974, 114 pp.

Virginia Lee Lussier, "National Faculty Associations in Collective Bargaining: A Comparative Discussion," ACBIS Special Report no. 8 (June, 1974) 21 pp.

Henry L. Mason, "Faculty Unionism and University Governance," in Jack H. Schuster, ed., Encountering the Unionized University. New Directions for Higher Education no. 5 (Spring, 1974) 1-26.

Bernard Mintz and Allan Golden, "Faculty Collective Bargaining and the Arbitral Process," CUPA Journal, 25 (July-August, 1974) 33-39.

Caesar J. Naples, "Collective Bargaining: Opportunities for 'Management'," in Jack H. Schuster, ed., Encountering the Unionized University. New Directions for Higher Education no. 5 (Spring, 1974) 47-60.

Caesar J. Naples, "Collegiality and Collective Bargaining: They Belong Together," NCSCBHE Proceedings, 2nd Annual Conference, (April, 1974) 51-57.

Robert L. Sawicki, "The Unionization of Professors at the University of Delaware," Liberal Education, 60 (December, 1974) 449-460; also

Jack H. Schuster, ed., Encountering the Unionized University. New Directions for Higher Education no. 5 (Spring, 1974) 106 pp.

Elizabeth Ward, "Libraries and Unions, the Saint Mary's University Experience," Canadian Library Journal (June, 1974) 238-240.

John Weatherford, "Librarians in Faculty Unions," Library Journal, 99 (October 1, 1974) 2443-2446.

1975

Trevor Bain, "Academic Governance and Unions: The Case of CUNY," Industrial Relations, 14 (February, 1975) no. 1, 102-109.

James P. Begin, Theodore Settle, and Paula Alexander, Academics on Strike. Institute of Management and Labor Relations (Rutgers), and ACBIS, 1975, 135 pp.

Dora Biblartz, et al., "Professional Associations and Unions: Future Impact of Today's Decisions," College and Research Libraries, (March, 1975) 121-127.

Thomas A. Brown, "Have Collective Negotiations Increased Teachers' Salaries?" Journal of Collective Negotiations in the Public Sector, 4 (1975) no. 1, 53-66.

Mary Anne Burns and Jeanette Carter, "Collective Bargaining and Faculty Status for Librarians: West Chester State College," College and Research Libraries, 36 (March, 1975) 115-120.

Anne Commerton, "Union or Professional Organization? A Librarian's Dilemma," College and Research Libraries, 36 (March, 1975) 129-135.

Herman Doh, "Collective Bargaining in SUNY: The Story of the Senate Professional Association," CUPA Journal, 25 (January, 1975), 22-39.

Thomas Emmet and Doris Ross, "1975 Legislative Activity: Progress Report on Postsecondary Collective Negotiation Bills," ACBIS Special Report no. 21 (April, 1975) 8 pp.

Michael A. Falcone, "Collective Bargaining: Its Effects on Campus Governance," ACBIS Special Report no. 16 (February, 1975) 6 pp.

Susan Fratkin, "Collective Bargaining and Affirmative Action," CUPA Journal, 26 (July-August, 1975) no. 3, 53-62.

Joseph Garbarino and Bill Aussieker, Faculty Bargaining: Change and Conflict. A Report Prepared for the Carnegie Commission on Higher Education and the Ford Foundation. McGraw-Hill, 1975, 278 pp.

Frank R. Kemerer and J. Victor Baldridge, Faculty Collective Bargaining and Academic Governance. Stanford Center for Research and Development in Teaching. MS for publication.

Seymour M. Lipset, "Faculty Unions and Collegiality," Change, 7 (March, 1975) 39-41.

Cecily Johns Little, "Faculty Status and Collective Bargaining," Michigan Librarian, 41 (Fall, 1975) no. 7, 10-12.

Thomas Mannix, "Prospective Issues at the Bargaining Table," ACBIS Special Report no. 19 (March, 1975) 6 pp.

Gary A. Moore, "... Comment," Journal of Collective Negotiations in the Public Sector, 4 (1975) no. 3, 253-256.

Kenneth P. Mortimer, "A Survey of Experience in Academic Collective Bargaining." Paper presented at ACRL, San Francisco, June 27, 1975, 21 pp.

Kenneth P. Mortimer, et al., Faculty Voting Behavior in the Temple University Collective Bargaining Elections. Center for the Study of Higher Education, Pennsylvania State University, 1975, 61 pp.

E. Reuben and L. Hoffman, ed., Unladylike and Unprofessional: Academic Women and Academic Unions. Modern Language Association, 1975, 54 pp.

Lothar Spang, "Collective Bargaining and University Librarians: Wayne State University," College and Research Libraries, 36 (March, 1975) 106-114.

Paul Strohm, "Faculty Input May Not Equal Output," Chronicle of Higher Education, 9 (February 10, 1975) 24.

Terrence N. Tice, ed., Campus Employment Relations: Readings and Resources. Ann Arbor, Institute for Continuing Legal Education, 1975, 627 pp.

John W. Weatherford, "Professional Associations and Bargaining Agents," Library Journal, 100 (January 15, 1975) 99-101.

John W. Weatherford, "Participatory Something or Other Through Bargaining," Library Journal, 100 (May 1, 1975) 823-825.

Background: Colleges and Universities

"Academic Freedom and Tenure, Statement of Principles, 1940," AAUP Bulletin, 27 (February, 1941) 40-45. Also

William G. Bowen, "The Effects of Inflation/Recession on Higher Education," Educational Record, 56 (Summer, 1975) 149-155.

Neil S. Bucklew, "Unionized Students on Campus," Educational Record, 54 (Fall, 1973) 300.

Commission on Academic Tenure in Higher Education, Faculty Tenure. Jossey-Bass, 1973, 276 pp.   Also

"Council Position on Collective Bargaining," AAUP Bulletin, (Spring, 1972) 46-61.

Harold L. Hodgkinson, The Campus Senate: Experiment in Democracy. Center for Research and Development in Higher Education, 1974, 151 pp.

George Louis Joughin, Academic Freedom and Tenure.   U. of Wisconsin, 1967, 343 pp.

Dwight R. Ladd, "Myths and Realities of University Governance," College and Research Libraries, 36 (March, 1975) 97-105.

"1968 Recommended Institutional Regulations on Academic Freedom and Tenure," AAUP Bulletin, 54 (Winter, 1968) 448-452.

"Statement on Faculty Workload," AAUP Bulletin, 52 (Winter, 1966) 385-386.

"Statement on Government of Colleges and Universities," AAUP Bulletin, 52 (Winter, 1966) 375-379.

"Two Steps Backward.   Report on the Economic Status of the Profession, 1974-75," AAUP Bulletin, 61 (August, 1975) 119-199.   p. 127.

Robert L. Williams, The Administration of Academic Affairs in Higher Education.   U. of Michigan Press, 1965, 182 pp.   16-22.

Background: Librarians

Lawrence W. S. Auld, "ALA and Collective Bargaining," ALA Bulletin (January, 1969) 96-97.

William Axford, "An Overlooked Cost of Achieving a Participatory Environment," College and Research Libraries, 35 (January, 1974) 5-6.

Martha Boaz, "Labor Unions and Libraries," California Librarian, 32 (April-July, 1971) 104-108.

Donald F. Cameron and Peggy Heim, Librarians in Higher Education. Their Compensation Structure for the Academic Year 1972-73. Council on Library Resources, 1974, 24 pp.

"Collective Bargaining: Questions and Answers," ALA Bulletin, 62 (December 1968) 1385-1390.

Richard De Gennaro, "Participative Management or Unionization?" College and Research Libraries, 33 (May, 1972) 173-174.

Harry R. Gates, "The Academic Status Illusion and the Nine-month Contract," Pacific Northwest Library Association Quarterly, (Winter, 1972) 3-6.

Theodore Lewis Guyton, Unionization: The Viewpoint of Librarians. A.L.A., 1975, 204 pp.

Carl Hintz, "Criteria for Appointment to and Promotion in Academic Rank," College and Research Libraries, 29 (September, 1968) 341-346. Also

Ed Holley, "Who Runs Libraries? The Emergence of Library Governance in Higher Education," Wilson Library Bulletin, 48 (September, 1973) 42-50.

"Joint Statement on Faculty Status of College and University Librarians," College and Research Libraries News (September, 1973) 209-212.

Louis Kaplan, "The Literature of Participation: From Optimism to Realism," College and Research Libraries, 36 (November, 1975) 473-479.

David Kaser, "Modernizing the University Library Structure," College and Research Libraries, 31 (July, 1970) 227-231.

Beverly Lynch, "Participative Management in Relation to

Library Effectiveness," College and Research Libraries, 33 (September, 1972) 384.

Virgil F. Massman, Faculty Status for Librarians. Scarecrow, 1972, 229 pp.

"Model Statement of Criteria and Procedures for Appointment, Promotion in Academic Rank, and Tenure for College and University Librarians," College and Research Libraries News, (September, 1973) 192-195.

J. Carlyle Parker, "Faculty Status and the Academic Work Year," California Librarian, 33 (July, 1972) 143-149.

Gail Schlachter, "Quasi Unions and Organizational Hegemony within the Library Field," Library Quarterly, 43 (July, 1973) 185-198.

C. James Schmidt, "Salary Plans for Academic Librarians...," Protean, 2 (Summer, 1972) 22-25.

Eldred Smith, "Librarians and Unions: The Berkeley Experience," Library Journal (February 15, 1968) 717-720.

Dennis Stone, "The Prospect of Unionism," American Libraries, 5 (July-August, 1974) 364-366.

Adeline Tallau and Benjamin R. Beede, "Faculty Status and Library Governance," Library Journal, 99 (June 1, 1974) 1521-1523.

Background: Employee Relations

Richard Bronstein, "Cost of Living and Salary Administration," Personnel, 52 (March-April, 1975) 11-18.

Audrey Freedman, "Cost-of-Living Clauses in Collective Bargaining," Michigan Business Review, 27 (January, 1975) 6-11.

Marie R. Haug and Marvin B. Sussman, "Professionalization and Unionism, a Jurisdictional Dispute?" American Behavioral Scientist, 15 (March-April, 1971) 528.

James J. Healy, ed., Creative Collective Bargaining. Prentice-Hall, 1965, 294 pp. 14.

J. David Kerr, "Pending Federal Legislation Providing State Public Employee Collective Bargaining," paper presented at the National Association of College and University Administrators, 1975. Processed, 16 pp.

Maurice P. Marchant, "Participative Management as Related to Personnel Development," Library Trends, 20 (July, 1971) 49.

National Education Association, Government Relations, Legislative Analysis. "Collective Bargaining for Public Employees... H. R. 77 (March 25, 1975)." Processed, 3 pp.

Arthur A. Sloane and Fred Witney, Labor Relations. 2nd edition, Prentice-Hall, 1972, 554 pp. 395.

Russell A. Smith, Harry T. Edwards, and R. Theodore Clark, Labor Relations Law in the Public Sector, Bobbs Merrill, 1974, 1222.

Donald Wollett and Robert Chanin, Law and Practice of Teacher Negotiations. Bureau of National Affairs, 1970.

Principal Collective Bargaining
Agreements Consulted

The following list contains those bargained agreements consulted in the course of research for this book. The affiliate is included, rather than the formal name of the particular bargaining agent. Dates listed are expiration dates for the agreement. All are faculty union agreements except Claremont.

Adelphi University (AAUP) 1976

Bard College (AAUP) 1974

Boston State College (AFT) 1975

Central Michigan University (NEA) 1971; 1974; 1977.

City University of New York (AFT) 1975

Claremont Colleges (OPEIU) 1974

Eastern Michigan University (AAUP) 1976

Fairleigh Dickinson University (AAUP) 1976

Ferris State College (NEA) 1975

Fitchburg State College (NEA) 1976

Hofstra University (AAUP) 1976

Lowell State College (AFT) 1976

Massachusetts College of Art (AFT) 1975

Monmouth College (NEA) 1976

New Jersey Institute of Technology (independent union) 1976

New Jersey State Colleges (AFT) 1976

Oakland University (AAUP) 1972; 1975

Pennsylvania State Colleges (NEA) 1977

Rhode Island College (AFT) 1975

Rider College (AAUP) 1976

Rutgers University (AAUP) 1973; 1975

Saginaw Valley College (NEA) 1975

St. John's University (AAUP) 1974

Southeastern Massachusetts University (AFT) 1976

State University of New York (NEA/AFT) 1974; 1976

Temple University (AAUP) 1976

University of Delaware (AAUP) 1975

University of Rhode Island (AAUP) 1975

Wayne State University (AAUP) 1976

Worcester State College (AFT) 1975

Youngstown State University (NEA) 1975

NATIONAL LABOR RELATIONS BOARD
UNIT DETERMINATIONS

Generally it does not seem useful to repeat legal citations from the footnotes. It might be helpful, however, to
cite relevant NLRB unit determinations in Labor Relations
Reference Manual. Bureau of National Affairs. (Vol. 1,
1935-37-). It should be remembered that units so

determined do not necessarily enter into bargaining, and
that many units are determined by others than NLRB.

74 LRRM 1269 Cornell University

77 LRRM 1001 and 1006 Long Island University

78 LRRM 1177 Fordham University

78 LRRM 1273 University of Detroit

79 LRRM 1253 Manhattan College

79 LRRM 1545 Adelphi University

80 LRRM 1160 Florida Southern University

81 LRRM 1317 Claremont Colleges

81 LRRM 1345 Tusculum College

82 LRRM 1385 Catholic University of America Law School

83 LRRM 1549 New York University

83 LRRM 1373 Syracuse University

84 LRRM 1033 Fairleigh-Dickinson University

84 LRRM 1163 Loretto Heights College

84 LRRM 1403 University of San Francisco Law School

MISCELLANEOUS PROCESSED MATERIALS

CUNY:

  Board of Higher Education of the City of New York.
Index, Digest, and Tables of Arbitration and Court Cases...
Vol. 1: Cases Decided September 1, 1969 through January
31, 1974. National Center for the Study of Collective Bargaining in Higher Education, 1974. 216 pp.

Oakland University:

  In the Matter of Arbitration between Oakland University ... and the American Association of University Professors. (Aug., 1973). 12 pp.

SUNY, Oswego:

  By-Laws of the Library Department, Penfield Library
Faculty, SUNY at Oswego (June 11, 1974).

U. of California, Berkeley:

University Council, American Federation of Teachers. A Library Improvement Program for the University of California. Draft (Feb. 1, 1973).

United Federation of Librarians. Library Improvement Program, University of California, Berkeley (Aug. , 1968). 14 pp.

INDEX

143